I0426451

More
PRAISE
of
PHRASES

More
PRAISE
of
PHRASES

*A second collection of amusing and
surprising stories behind our familiar sayings,
clichés, catchphrases, and proverbs*

JOHN PETERSON

WiSP
PRESS

© 2013 WiSP Press

Design & Cover Illustration by Ted Schluenderfritz

ISBN: 978-1493565207

Dedicated to Joan, my wife, and
To Joan, my sweetheart, and
To Joan my partner in every endeavor

Table of Contents

The people and events behind our familiar sayings

The people and events behind our familiar sayings

Author's Note

A S I MENTIONED IN MY "INTRODUCTION" TO VOLUME I OF this series, the inspiration for these stories about phrases and their origins was a comment by the British journalist-philosopher G.K. Chesterton written back in 1908: "Half our speech consists of similes that remind us of no similarity," he wrote, "of pictorial phrases that call up no picture, and of historical allusions the origin of which we have forgotten." When I read this I had recently been rather startled by learning that "God willing and the Creek don't rise" did not refer to a stream flooding but rather to the Creek Indian Federation rising in rebellion against the settlers. I wondered if there were more such stories.

I learned there are countless such stories and so I began to collect them. The results of my searches are presented in this book and its predecessor, *In Praise of Phrases*.

As I also noted in the first volume, I did not intend these researches of mine to contribute anything original to the academic disciplines known as etymology and lexicography. I had no doubt that experts, if any are interested, will find errors of fact in my narratives. That will not trouble me, for my simple purpose is more to amuse my readers rather than to educate them.

—*John Peterson*

The Phrases

"We have met the enemy and he is us."

WALT KELLY (1913–1973)

R EADERS WHO DID NOT FOLLOW THE COMIC STRIPS during the previous century will probably believe this is a foolish misquotation. They will remind us that General (and later, President) William Henry Harrison (1773–1841) famously wrote (in 1813) that "We have met the enemy and they are ours." He was referring to his victory in the Battle of Lake Erie during the War of 1812.

Fans of the comics, however, will know that the statement accurately quotes the late cartoonist Kelly, whose long-running comic strip *Pogo* captivated adults and children alike. The title of the strip, they will remind us, refers to the leading character, friendly "Pogo Possum," whose adventures in the Okefenokee Swamp represented a new era of sophistication in comic strips. Memorable characters in *Pogo* included Pogo's cigar-smoking sidekick Albert Alligator, the educator of the series Howland Owl (who always and laughably had his facts entirely wrong), and the superstitious Churchy LaFemme, the swamp's self-styled poet.

There were many collections of the Pogo strips published during Kelly's lifetime, and the final one (released just before the cartoonist's death in 1973) bore the title, "We have met the enemy and he is us."

"Star-Spangled Banner."

FRANCIS SCOTT KEY (1779–1843)

THE NAME OF FRANCIS SCOTT KEY WILL BE FOREVER associated with our national anthem (at least for Americans who are left with some knowledge of national history). Key was a lawyer, author, and something of an amateur poet. The occasion that inspired his one memorable poem took place during the War of 1812 when Key boarded the British warship *Tonnant* to negotiate an exchange of prisoners. While aboard, he watched the nighttime bombardment of Fort McHenry in September of 1814. When the sun rose, Key could see that the American flag was still flying over the fort. This inspired him to write a poem celebrating the event—a poem he entitled "The Defense of Fort McHenry."

The poem was published under that name in *The Patriot* in September of 1914, and included these memorable lines:

> Oh say does that star-spangled banner yet wave
> O'er the land of the free and the home of the brave?

In 1916, President Woodrow Wilson ordered the song adopted as the American national anthem, under the name "The Star Spangled Banner." In 1931 a Congressional resolution signed by President Herbert Hoover made the song the official anthem of the United States. Other popular names for the flag include "Old Glory," "The Stars and Stripes," and "The Red, White and Blue."

The flag had been designed by Francis Hopkinson (an author and signer of the Declaration of Independence) and was approved by act of Congress in 1777. The story that seamstress Betsy Ross made the first of these flags has been discredited.

"*Playing hooky.*"

MARK TWAIN (1835–1910)

MOST READERS ALREADY KNOW THAT "MARK TWAIN" was the penname of Samuel Langhorn Clemens, the nineteenth-century American humorist and author whose most famous works were the novels *The Adventures of Tom Sawyer* (1876) and *The Adventures of Huckleberry Finn* (1885). However, those readers may not also know that Clemens' penname "Mark Twain" was derived from his years as a Mississippi riverboat pilot and the depth soundings regularly announced to warn pilots when the river was becoming dangerously shallow: "Mark on the Twine! Ten fathoms!"

The word "Hooky" is derived from the Dutch "*hoekje*" ("hide"). And of course "playing hooky" today means "to skip school." The phrase's first appearance in print traces to *Tom Sawyer*: "He moped to school gloomy and sad, and took his flogging, along with Joe Harper, for playing hooky the day before."

We are further informed, by those who trace phrase histories, that "hooky" was originally derived from "by hook or by crook" (meaning "by any means—whether honest or dishonest").

"One-horse town."

MARK TWAIN (1835–1910)

Samuel Langhorne Clemens, or Mark Twain, led a colorful life, but in addition to his adventures and writings, his legacy should also include some admirable quotes. Here are just a few:

Suppose you were an idiot, and suppose you were a member of Congress. But I repeat myself.

Those newspaper reports of my death were greatly exaggerated.

Be respectful to your superiors—if you have any.

A circle is a round straight line with a hole in the middle.

Heaven for climate. Hell for society.

The difference between the *almost right* word and the *right* word is the difference between 'lightning-bug' and 'lightning.'

Honesty is the best policy when there is money in it.

If you don't read the newspaper you are uninformed, if you do read the newspaper you are misinformed.

I am opposed to millionaires, but it would be dangerous to offer me the position.

First get your facts, and then you can distort them at your leisure.

A classic—something that everybody wants to have read and nobody wants to read.

Thunder is good, thunder is impressive; but it is lightning that does the work.

The lack of money is the root of all evil.

The only reason why God created man is because he was disappointed with the monkey.

A man is never more truthful than when he acknowledges himself a liar.

There is no distinctly native American criminal class except Congress.

Last, one of our very small and backward villages was labeled by Twain as "that poor little one-horse town." (And we note that the phrase "One-Horse Town" also gave songwriter Bernie Taupin the title for a 1976 Elton John hit song.)

"It went over like a lead balloon."

WOODSON MESSICK COWAN (1889–1977)

THIS SAYING, NOW A TIRED CLICHÉ, WAS COINED BY cartoonist "Wood" Cowan back in 1924. His early newspaper comic strip, *Mom 'n Pop*, now entirely forgotten by even our oldest readers, had Pop investing in a company called "Consolidated Mothballs." Unfortunately for Pop, the stock "was about to go up as fast as a lead balloon."

The phrase did not catch on at the time, and it was not until after World War II that "lead balloon" became popular with newspaper writers and readers.

This inevitably brings us to the music of the 1960's and the popular heavy-metal band Led Zeppelin. Was there an echo of "lead balloon" in this name? Indeed, members of the band confirmed in a number of interviews that the group got its name in response to the cynical prediction that success would elude them, and they would "go down like a lead balloon."

"Beat around the bush."

GEORGE GASCOIGNE (1535–1577)

T O UNDERSTAND THIS ONE, WE HAVE TO REVIEW BIRD hunting in Gascoigne's day. Some members of the hunting party (called "beaters") literally beat the bushes to flush out the birds nesting or otherwise hiding there. The others were ready with nets to snare the birds as they took flight from the bushes. In fact, beaters are still used in today's bird hunts. Thus we have this meaning: "any activity prior to the main event."

Gascoigne was an English poet with a reputation in his own day for being innovative. After his studies at Cambridge, he served as a Member of Parliament and a soldier in the military. It is in his *Collected Works* of 1572 that we find the first published reference to this phrase: "He beat about the bush while others caught the birds." Today the phrase is used to show impatience with someone's failure to get to an activity's main event or to get to the point of a meandering conversation.

"Grease my palm."

JOHN SKELTON (C. 1460–1529)

T HIS, IT TURNS OUT, IS A VERY OLD SAYING AND VERY widely used (the French say *"graisser la patte"*). It means, of course, to bribe or at least to give someone like the restaurant's host or hostess a gratuity for quickly finding your party a table; and it invites comparison with the more literal uses of grease: to make things run smoothly as in "greasing the wheels" or "greasing the skids."

We use "elbow grease" to get our work done, we hire a "grease monkey" to work on our automobiles in a "grease pit," we note that something is very fast when we say it goes like "greased lightning," and it is not considered high praise when we describe a restaurant as a "greasy spoon" or when our hair is said to be full of "greasy kid stuff." Finally, we have those "greasers" (tough guys on motorcycles).

John Skelton (sometimes referred to as John Shelton) was an English poet who also wrote three plays, the script for just one of which, *Magnificence*, has survived. Here for the record is the earliest known appearance of our phrase about "greasing":

> Thus am I occupied at all assays
> Whatsoever I do all men praise
> And make ill am I made nowadays
> Counterfeit matters in the law of the land
> With gold and grotes they grease my hand
> Instead of right that wrong may stand.

We note in passing that in the North and West, "greasy" is pronounced with an "S" sound ("greeSSy") and in middle America and in the South, it is pronounced with a "Z" sound ("greeZZy").

"Until Hell freezes over."

ADLAI STEVENSON II (1900–1965)

THIS PHRASE WAS NOT ORIGINATED BY GOVERNOR Stevenson, for it is found in profusion in former times and around the world today. Due to our lexicographers' inability to pin down the origination of the phrase, we turn to Stevenson as the one who used it most memorably and dramatically.

During what we now refer to as "The Cuban missile crisis" of 1962, Stevenson , then the American ambassador to the United Nations, challenged the Russian ambassador, Valarian Zorin, by demanding he answer "yes or no" to his question about the presence of Russian missiles in Cuba. When Zorin refused to answer, Stevenson reponded with, "I am prepared to wait for my answer until Hell freezes over." Stevenson then showed photographs proving that Russian missile silos were indeed present in Cuba.

Other popular phrases about the temperature in hell include, "A cold day in hell," "not a snowball's chance in hell," and even "when the Devil goes ice skating." One of the ironies of all this is that in many cultures, Hell is depicted as a barren wasteland of snow and ice, and even within the Christian tradition we have Dante's depiction of the lowest circle of Hell (in "The Inferno" of his *Divine Comedy*) as a frozen lake reserved for the traitors.

Finally, this: about thirty miles northwest of Detroit lies the little town of Hell, Michigan. All through the winter, local radio stations make a note of the day when Hell freezes over.

"The peanut gallery."

EDWARD H. KNIGHT (??–1883)

HE EARLIEST USE OF THIS PHRASE, USED TO DESCRIBE A theater's cheapest seats, surprises us not only because it is very early but because it is found in a technical dictionary. In E.H. Knight's *Practical Dictionary of Mechanics* (1877), we read about the "syrinx," a nose-making instrument resembling panpipes. The Roman audiences employed these to show displeasure (the syrinx replaced hissing because it produced a much louder sound). Knight traced the use of such devices to what he referred to as the "peanut galleries" of those ancient times.

Why "peanut"? We're told that in the days of vaudeville, the cheapest snacks were peanuts and the cheapest seats were in the balconies at the theater's rear. Patrons of the "cheap seats" would heckle performers and even throw peanuts at them to show their disapproval.

In more recent times, those who passively observe the various internet social websites are also referred to as a peanut gallery.

"Carry him piggyback."

JAMES CALFHILL (1530?–1570)

E CAN PICTURE A SMALL GIRL CARRYING HER LITTLE brother in piggyback fashion, his arms around her neck and her arms at her sides, holding the fellow with her elbows around his knees. But what in the world does this have to do with pigs? Well, originally, the phrase was "pack-a-back," meaning "carried on the back or shoulders" as a pack is carried.

James Calfhill was an English clergyman educated at Cambridge. A strict Calvinist, his major work was the polemical *Answer to the Treatise of the Crosse* (1565), which condemned the ideas of Bishop Richard Cheyney.

Cheyney had defended the Crucifix displayed in Queen Mary's chapel. Calfhill, then, ridiculed the idea that "The way to heaven whereto we may be carried pack-a-back on a Rood [Cross]." That notion, according to Calfhill makes things "too easy" for the Christian.

We do not know exactly how or when "pack-a-back" became "piggyback," except for the similarity in the sound of the phrases and "pack-a-back" perhaps did not seem to apply when the object carried was not a pack but a person.

"Red line."

WILLIAM H. RUSSELL (1820–1907)

*J*OURNALISTS AND POLITICIANS OF LATE HAVE TAKEN TO using the phrase "red line" to indicate the point at which hostilities are certain to break out. For example, an Associated Press headline informed us early in 2012 that "Troops from Chad draw red line for rebels in the Central African Republic of Damara." At about the same time, a *Washington Post* headline declared that, "Americans see chemical weapon 'red line' in Syria," and Marc Ambinder of *The Week* declared that, according to Israeli Prime Minister Benjamin Netanyahu, Israel's line will start flashing red when Iran's nuclear program approaches the point of bomb production.

We used to say "draw a line in the sand" to mean the point that if passed would precipitate a war or at least some sort of fight. That idea dates back to the second century BC, when a Roman ambassador drew a circle in the sand around Antiochus IV, ruler of the Seleucid Empire. So the question becomes, where did we get "red line" and why is it *red*?

William Howard Russell was a fun-loving London journalist born in Ireland and educated in Dublin. As a reporter for the *London Times*, he was dispatched to various warfronts including the Battle of Balaclava in 1854.

Regarding that battle, Russell described the formation of the ninety-third Highlanders of the British infantry as "the thin red line" because they did not have sufficient numbers to station second and third lines behind their front line. The Highlanders were so taken with this representation that they later named their regimental magazine *The Thin Red Line*. And we remember that the American colonists referred to British soldiers as "redcoats."

Unfortunately, the question of how or why the phrase resurfaced among today's journalists and politicians is an elusive one. Of course in ice hockey the goalkeeper is not allowed to cross the red line at center ice, but that does not appear to be the source of the phrase's popularity today. Nor does it seem related to "redlining," the practice of mortgage lenders who outline on a map the neighborhoods in which the residents are not considered good credit risks.

"Up! Up! And away!"

BEN PETER FREEMAN (1901–1992)

*I*N FREEMAN'S RADIO SCRIPTS FOR THE *SUPERMAN* SHOW, THE "Man of Steel" shouted these words as he prepared to leap tall buildings in a single bound or otherwise fly about. What is so interesting about Superman on the radio is that the comic-book version of Superman that introduced our first super hero in 1938 was almost entirely visual in its appeal. We saw bullets bouncing off of Superman's chest. He saw him pick up automobiles and toss them about. We watched as his x-ray vision revealed what was going on behind those impenetrable brick walls.

As to the radio version, we saw nothing except what our imaginations revealed as suggested by the radio narrative and dialogue. And that brings us to Freeman, the writer who was responsible for the radio scripts and for bringing the adventures of "the Man of Tomorrow" to life in the imaginations of the listeners. He had the help of sound effects, of course, including most memorably the whooshing sound of Superman's excursions through the skies ("Look! Up in the sky! It's a bird! It's a plane! It's Superman!")

The show was a huge success, airing daily in the late afternoon (after school, of course), until the advent of television which wedded the persona of actor Steve Reeves to that of Superman.

Those who were tuned into popular music during the 1960's might have expected to read here about The Fifth Dimension, the singing group that made the charts with their single "Up, Up and Away":

> If you'll hold my hand we'll chase your dream across the sky
> For we can fly we can fly
> Up, up and away
> In my beautiful, my beautiful balloon

"The thrill of victory and the agony of defeat."

STANLEY RALPH ROSS (1935–2000)

THE NAME OF THE LATE JIM MCKAY (BORN JAMES MCMANUS) is the one remembered as the voice of *ABC's Wide World of Sports*, which aired from 1961 through 1998. The program offered television's sports fans a break from their steady diet of baseball, football, and basketball by showcasing special events (such as the Kentucky Derby, for example, or the Indianapolis 500, Wimbledon tennis, and the British Open golf tournament.) It was McKay's opening announcement that is so well remembered by television's sports fans: "Spanning the globe to bring you the constant variety of sport: the thrill of victory and the agony of defeat, the human drama of athletic competition. This is *ABC's Wide World of Sports!*"

McKay's words were scripted by Stanley Ross, a Brooklyn adman who later worked as a television script writer for a number of ABC's programs including *Batman, The Monkees, All in the Family,* and many others.

Readers may find the inscription on Ross's gravestone of interest: "Beloved Son, Husband, Father, Grandfather; July 22, 1935–March 16, 2000. Thanks, I Had A Wonderful Time!"

"Not my cup of tea."

ALFRED ALISTAIR COOKE (1908–2004)

O F COURSE TEA IS THE BRITISH HOT DRINK OF CHOICE, EASILY surpassing even the American love for hot coffee. And so we can understand the comparisons, "He's my cup of tea" or "That is really not my cup of tea." We use these expressions in the USA now, largely because of Alistair Cook's influence.

Cook is probably best remembered today as the perennial host of our Public Broadcasting's programming series, *Masterpiece Theater*. His other signature program, *Letter from America*, was broadcast worldwide for nearly sixty years (surely some sort of record for longevity). That is where (in 1944) he explained that in England, "You don't say someone gives you a pain in the neck. You just remark 'He's not my cup of tea.'" We Americans have been using this metaphor ever since.

And here is the place for a brief historical note: in 1773, the citizens of Boston (disguised as Native Americans) raided three British ships and dumped several hundred chests of tea into the harbor to protest the taxes and monopoly of the East India Company. The event, remembered by us as "The Boston Tea Party," eventually led to the American War for Independence.

"Me Tarzan. You Jane."

DAVID IVOR DAVIES (1893–1951)

YOUNGER READERS MAY HAVE NO IDEA OF WHO SOMEONE named "Tarzan" might have been or why he deserves our interest today. Older readers, on the other hand, though they will not remember author Edgar Rice Burroughs' novel *Tarzan of the Apes* (1914), they may recall the numerous spinoffs into movies, comic books, and a newspaper comic strip. The premise? As an infant Tarzan was the sole survivor of an airplane crash in the African jungle. He was then raised by a family of apes as one of their own.

Swimming champion Johnny Weissmuller (1904–1984) is most famously remembered for his portrayal of the Tarzan character in eleven feature films. Weissmuller had won five Olympic gold medals in swimming during the 1920's. However, those who remember him today think of the Tarzan films in which he starred during the 1930's and '40's. Because Weissmuller was not an actor, script writer Davies gave him few lines, and these consisted of the short, primitive statements remembered today as "Me Tarzan. You Jane." The actual dialogue was somewhat different:

> Jane: (*pointing to herself*) Jane.
> Tarzan: Jane.
> Jane: And you? You?
> Tarzan: Tarzan, Tarzan.
> Jane: Tarzan.
> Tarzan: Jane. Tarzan. Jane. Tarzan...

Davies was better known by his professional name, David Novello. He was a popular British entertainer, songwriter, and stage actor during the first half of the twentieth century. After he turned to film acting, he was enlisted to script the first of the Weissmuller Tarzan films, *Tarzan the Ape Man* (1932). Actress Maureen O'Sullivan played Jane.

"Lame Duck."

HORACE WALPOLE (1717–1797)

*W*E SPEAK OF POLITICIANS WHO HAVE NOT BEEN reelected, or are not eligible for reelection, as "lame ducks." However, the term was first used to describe stock-market traders who were unsuccessful. It is clear enough why they were referred to as "lame"—they were impaired—but why "ducks"? Apparently, the reference is to the unfortunate duck that becomes a target for predators because it is too weak to keep up with its flock.

We must also note here that "duck" is a different, highly figurative, and much more useful word in the United Kingdom versus its more literal use by Americans. Brits use "ducky" as a synonym for "fine" or "excellent" as in "Everything is just ducky." It is also a term of friendliness or endearment, as in "Don't you agree, Ducky?" (Or, "Don't you agree, Ducks?")

In Walpole's day, incompetent stock traders who went bankrupt were called "lame ducks." The first published mention of the phrase appears as a question in Walpole's 1761 letter to the British diplomat Horace Mann: "Do you know what a Bull and a Bear and Lame Duck are?"

There are too many popular phrases with the word "duck" to list. Some of the more obvious are "dead duck," "sitting duck," "duck soup," "Lord, love a duck!" "duck out," "nibbled to death by ducks," "The Ugly Duckling" (Hans Christian Anderson's fairy tale), and the cartoon characters Donald Duck, Daffy Duck, and many others.

We also have the verb "to duck" (to avoid). The words for both that "duck" and the bird "duck" were derived from the same Middle English verb, *douken*, "to dive."

"Through thick and thin."

GEOFFREY CHAUCER (1343–1400)

WE STILL USE THIS VERY OLD SAYING WITH ITS OBVIOUS meaning of perseverance in spite of every sort of obstacle. Many, however, will be surprised to learn of the very literal meaning the phrase had originally. It referred to the difficulties travelers suffered in earlier centuries while journeying through the heavily wooded English countryside with its forests and wet flatlands ("fens").

Chaucer, "the Father of English Literature," is most remembered for his collection of stories, *The Canterbury Tales*, which gave the English language new respect as a legitimate vehicle for serious literature (versus Latin and French).

It is within "The Reeve's Tale" (a "reeve" was a bailiff) that our expression first appears:

> And whan the hors was laus, he gynneth gon
> Toward the fen, ther wilde mares renne,
> And forth with "wehee," thurgh thikke and thurgh thenne.
> [*And forth with "We-Hee," through thick and through thin.*]

We note in passing that the twentieth-century American comedian Jimmy Durante, renowned for his mangling of the King's English, recalled (of his early days as a jazz musician) that, "In those days we went through a lot of thicks and thins."

"A harbinger of things to come."

GEOFFREY CHAUCER (1343–1400)

S I WATCHED A TELEVISION NEWS PROGRAM, I HEARD one of the commentators use this phrase. I also recalled hearing (and probably saying), "harbinger of doom," "harbinger of spring," and more. But *harbinger*? What on earth is a *harbinger*?

Well, the word is related to the verb "harbor," to shelter, as in "he harbored fugitives in his attic." And the relationship? We turn to Chaucer once again, for in his day, a harbinger was the proprietor of a lodging-house. It also came to mean a sort of scout who went ahead of an aristocratic group of travelers to secure lodging for them for the night. It was not a great leap, then, for the harbingers to be looked upon as sources of information about visitors to come. This is how Chaucer used the word in "The Man of Law's Tale" in his *Canterbury Tales*:

> The news through all the town was carried,
> How King Alla would come on pilgrimage,
> By harbingers that went before him.

Come to think of it, yesterday's harbinger was not that far removed from the "advance man" who arranges scheduling for today's dignitaries.

"*Blown to smithereens.*"

FRANCIS PETER PLOWDEN (1749–1829)

MANY OF US ARE COMFORTABLE WITH USING THIS phrase, which of course means "exploded into tiny bits." But what are "smithereens"? The word comes to us from the Irish (Gaelic) *smidirn* ("small fragments") with the added diminutive "-een"—"*smidirneen*." In English, it is always used in the plural (as is the word "suds"). And we note that this same Irish word also gave us "smidgen" as in, "I'll just have a smidgen [tiny portion] of pie, please."

Francis Plowden was prominent in the early nineteenth century as a defender of Irish Catholic emancipation under the rule of Great Britain. In 1810 he was forced to flee to France to avoid prosecution for libel.

In his three-volume treatise, *The History of Ireland* (1801–1810), Plowden was the first to bring our "exploding" phrase to the reading public. In this treatise he reported a threat that was made against an Englishman, a Mr. Pounden, as follows: "If you don't be off directly, by the ghost of William our deliverer, and by the orange we wear, we will break your carriage in smithereens and hough [cripple] your cattle and burn your house."

"Zig zag."

JONATHAN SWIFT (1667–1745)

*S*HORT STRAIGHT LINES SET AT ANGLES TO ONE ANOTHER ARE said to "zig zag." The phrase comes down to us from the Dutch and the Germans (see, for example, the German word *zickzack,* which was used to describe how the walls of fortification for castles were positioned). "Zig zag" later came to be used to describe any series of changes back and forth, as in "His argument zigged and zagged between fact and fiction," and "His jobs zig zag from physical labor to intellectual pursuits and back again."

The Anglo-Irish Author Jonathan Swift is best remembered today for his fictional *Gulliver's Travels* (1726) although during his life he was more known as a pamphleteer and a cleric who became Dean of St. Paul's Cathedral. The first published appearance of our phrase occurs in his poem, *My Lady's Lamentation* (1728):

> Who makes the best figure,
> The Dean or the digger
> And which is the best
> At cracking a jest—
> How proudly he talks
> Of zig zags and walks!

We note in conclusion that the often heard "You zigged when you should have zagged" was first spoken in the 1998 Hollywood film, *The Waterboy.*

"*Cloak and dagger.*"

CHARLES DICKENS (1812–1870)

IMAGINE A SHADOWY FIGURE, LURKING IN A DOORWAY, A dagger or short sword in one hand and his cloak wrapped around his other arm to ward off the dagger attacks of others. That is the literal meaning of this phrase, but its use also suggests the more general ideas of dramatic intrigue, deceit, secrecy, and treachery, especially in storytelling.

Charles Dickens was the most popular writer of England's nineteenth-century Victorian period, and his novels are now still read and enjoyed. His fifth novel, *Barnaby Rudge* (1881), however, is one of his lesser works and is rarely referenced today. Its story was set in the previous century (during the Gordon Riots of 1780). The novel interests us here because it contains the first reference in English literature to our phrase, "cloak and dagger."

> His servant brought in a very small scrap of dirty paper, on the inside whereof was inscribed in pretty large text these words: "A friend. Desiring of a conference. Immediate. Private."
>
> "Where in the name of the Gunpowder Plot did you pick up this?" asked his master.
>
> "It was given him by a person then waiting at the door," the man replied.
>
> "With a cloak and dagger?" asked Mr. Chester.

"*I'll eat my hat.*"

THOMAS BRIDGES (1719–1775)

RIDGES WAS A WINE MERCHANT, A BANKER, AND something of an author. His written works included plays, parodies, and stories. He was the first writer to have used the promise about eating one's hat, which, even though widely used ever since, seems an odd way of expressing the certainty of the truth of one's opinion.

It is in Bridges' spoof translation of the ancient Greek poet Homer's epic *The Iliad* that we find the earliest reference to one's hat as a meal:

> For though we tumble down the wall,
> And fire their rotten boats and all,
> I'll eat my hat, if Jove don't drop us,
> Or play some queer rogue's trick to stop us.

Finally, we note in passing that Victorian novelist Charles Dickens added something else to the meal in 1837 in his *Pickwick Papers*:

> "Well, if I knew as little of life as that, I'd eat my hat and swallow the buckle whole," said the clerical gentleman.
> "So would I," added the sporting one solemnly.

"Spitting image."

ALICE HEGAN RICE (1870–1942)

*H*AVE YOU ASSUMED, AS I ALWAYS DID, THAT THE "SPIT" in this phrase is a corruption of the word "spirit"? It surely seems reasonable to believe "She is the very spirit and image of Aunt Helen" became "She was the very spit and ..." But, no. The experts give us a completely different history of the phrase and its meaning. They tell us that "spit" really does mean "spit" as in "saliva."

As unlikely as it may seem to us, the idea is that one person so resembles another as to seem as though he or she were spat out of the other's mouth. Really. That idea is quite old and widespread. (as, for example, in the French *"C'est le portrait craché de son père"* ("He's the spitting portrait of his father").

Alice Rice was an American novelist whose one remembered work is *Mrs. Wiggs of the Cabbage Patch* (1901). It was dramatized for the stage and cinema, and film buffs might be familiar with the 1934 Hollywood production starring W.C. Fields. The novel gives us our first printed example of our catchphrase: "He's jes like his pa—the very spittin' image of him!"

"Elvis Has Left The Building."

HORACE LEE HOGAN (1916–2002)

E DON'T HEAR THIS STATEMENT MUCH THESE DAYS. Until recently it was used when something or anything had ended, as in "We would all like to continue this meeting far into the night, my friends, but Elvis has …"

It was Elvis Presley, of course, the singer who soared to fame with the combination of rhythm-and-blues and country music that we know as "rock and roll" (it was originally known as "rockabilly.") Audiences for Presley's concerts would typically stay after the concert was over, hoping for just one more Elvis encore. Hogan, acting as master of ceremonies, assured these audiences that the concert was finished: "Alright! Alright! Elvis has left the building. He left the stage and went out the backdoor with the policemen. He's gone."

Horace Hogan began as a radio announcer at an early age (he was sixteen). His main claim to fame was his country-music show, *Hayride*, which became the cornerstone of the country music industry in America. Besides Elvis, Hogan introduced his listeners to such country luminaries as Johnny Cash and Hank Williams. Hogan introduced Elvis with this: "Ladies and gentlemen, you've never heard of this young man before, but one day you'll be able to tell your children and grandchildren you heard musical history made tonight." How right he was!

"On the Q.T."

GEORGE MOORE (1852–1933)

*W*E LIKE ABBREVIATIONS—THERE'S "PDQ" (PRETTY darn quick), "COD" (cash on delivery), "St" and Apt) (street and apartment) , "AM" and "PM" (ante meridian and post meridian, or before noon and after noon) "Fed Ex" and "UPS" (Federal Express and United Parcel Service), " "Jan" (January...and the other months), abbreviations for every state in the union from Al to WY, and, well, this list could be extended to any length we wish.

George Moore was an artist, a critic, and the first on a lengthy list of Irish novelists. Our phrase first appeared in print in his 1884 novel *A Mummer's Wife*: "It will be possible to have one spree on the strict q.t."

However, the real fun of the phrase traces back to 1891 when "Ta ra ra boom de ay," a minstrel show number possibly familiar to some of our readers, was played in London to rapturous applause:

> A sweet Tuxedo girl you see,
> Queen of swell society,
> Fond of fun as fun can be
> When it's on the strict Q.T.
>
> Ta ra ra boom de ay
> My sweetheart's gone away
> And he is gone to stay
> Ta ra ra boom de ay.

We note in conclusion that the tagline for the 1997 film *L.A. Confidential*: "Off the record, on the QT and very hush-hush." (No need here to explain to movie-goers that "L.A." stands for Los Angeles.)

"For whom the bell tolls."

JOHN DONNE (1572–1631)

ONNE WAS A PROMINENT ENGLISH POET AND A Church of England cleric who rose to become Dean of St. Paul's Cathedral. His inclusion here provides an excuse to quote in full this beautiful passage from his *Devotions upon Emergent Conditions*, written while he was recovering from a nearly fatal illness.

> No man is an island, entire of itself; every man is a piece of the continent, a part of the main. If a clod be washed away by the sea, Europe is the less, as well as if a promontory were, as well as if a manor of thy friend's or of thine own were: any man's death diminishes me, because I am involved in mankind, and therefore never send to know for whom the bells tolls; it tolls for thee.

American novelist Ernest Hemmingway (1899–1961) used "For Whom the Bell Tolls" as the title for his 1940 novel of the Spanish Civil War, and the Trappist monk Thomas Merton (1915–1968) borrowed "No Man is an Island" for the title to his 1955 book of meditations.

"My bad."

WILLIAM SHAKESPEARE (1564–1616)

SHAKESPEARE WAS OUR GREATEST POET, OUR GREATEST playwright, and far and away our greatest phrase maker. (Just a small sample: As pure as the new driven snow, At one fell swoop, Come what may, Fight fire with fire, Good riddance, In a pickle, It will make your hair stand on end, The primrose path, The game is up, Too much of a good thing, Up in arms, Vanish into thin air, Tell truth and shame the Devil, Wild goose chase, and Woe is me.) However, it does not seem possible that a phrase that is of so recent a vintage as "My bad" could trace all the way back to Shakespeare's day.

"My bad" came into popular usage in the second half of the twentieth century with pickup basketball. It meant "Sorry, my mistake—blame me." In the 1995 movie *Clueless*, a character named Cher, riding a bicycle, swerves to avoid an accident. Cher says, "Whoops, my bad!" The cinema exposure gave the phrase a more widespread currency.

Nevertheless, Shakespeare had it first and with its contemporary meaning as well. In his "Sonnet 112" we find, "What care I who calls me well or ill, so you green over my bad?"

"In a Pickle."

WILLIAM SHAKESPEARE (1564–1616)

I N A "PICKLE"? WELL, IN TROUBLE: IN A BIND, IN A BOX, IN A stew, in a corner, in a fix, in a jam, in the dog house, in a tight spot, in a daze, in a hole, in a quandary, and many more.

The earliest citation known? Yes, it's Shakespeare again. In *The Tempest*, his final play (1610), we find:

> ALONSO: How camest thou in this pickle?
> TRINCULO: I have been in such a pickle since I saw you last.

And why "pickle"? The meaning is related to "in a stew" because both being stewed (cooked) and being pickled (seasoned in vinegar and brine) would seem to be far from a pleasant experience.

"*Keep your powder dry.*"

OLIVER CROMWELL (1599–1658)

ROMWELL ("OLD IRONSIDES") WAS AND IS A CONTROVERSIAL figure in British history, and that is an understatement at best. His oppressive policies against Catholics in Ireland are viewed as genocide by some. However, his defeat of the Irish in the Confederate Wars made him a hero to the British populace.

Before crossing a river to attack an enemy position, Cromwell reportedly instructed his troops to "put your trust in God, but mind to keep your powder dry." His obvious meaning was for the soldiers to protect their gunpowder from being soaked in the river's water. Today, "Keep your powder dry" has been generalized to mean "Conserve your resources until needed."

Other phrases about "powder" in popular use include "powder room" (a public rest room for women—the reference is to face powder), "powder blue" (a pale blue color), "take a powder" (leave quickly), and "powder monkey" (someone who handles explosives).

"Photo finish."

ALFRED DAMON RUNYON (1880–1946)

*W*E REMEMBER DAMON RUNYON TODAY (THOSE OF US who do remember him) as the writer whose short stories gave us the 1950 award-winning Broadway musical *Guys and Dolls* and the 1955 cinema version with Marlin Brando, Jean Simmons, and Frank Sinatra. It was Runyon's short stories that created for us his imagined world of Brooklyn and Broadway with its gamblers, gangsters, and other streetwise hustlers: Harry the Horse, Nathan Detroit, Benny Southstreet, Nicely-Nicely, and countless others.

We should further be reminded that Runyon was also a serious newspaper reporter, assigned by United Press, for example, the task of covering Franklin President Roosevelt's inauguration in 1933.

Racing's "photo finish" refers to a dead heat ending, resolved by referring to a photograph snapped at the finish line at the exact conclusion of the race Although the phrase was already quite familiar to racing fans, Runyon introduced it to the reading public in his 1938 story, "Take It Easy": "I will take Nicely-Nicely against anything on four legs, except maybe an elephant, and at that he may give the elephant a photo finish."

We quickly add that, as any office manager will briefly explain, "photo-finishing" is an entirely unrelated activity.

"Gone cuckoo."

HOWARD VINCENT O'BRIEN (1888–1947)

O F COURSE THE CUCKOO IS THAT REAL BIRD, KNOWN FOR placing its eggs in the nests of other birds and leaving for them the task of nesting until all of the eggs are hatched. (Incidentally, this is the reason we refer to the husband of an unfaithful wife as a "cuckold.") The cuckoo is also the toy bird that emerges from the so-called "cuckoo clock" to announce the passing of the hours.

But why "crazy"? It is the seemingly senseless repetition of the cuckoo's peculiar call (sometimes spelled "coo-coo!") that is apparently without any purpose and without any purposeful result (or so it seems to most observers). The 1950's gave us the shortened version, "kook" and "kooky."

Howard O'Brien was an American novelist, editor, and columnist for the *Chicago Daily News*. His best known work was his anonymous 1926 memoir, *Wine, Women and War*. There we find the first reference in print to "cuckoo" as crazy: "Wish my daughter would grow up. She certainly must have been cuckoo!"

We must also reference *One Flew over the Cuckoo's Nest*, the 1975 film starring Jack Nicholson (in which the "cuckoo's nest" was an insane asylum); and ancient Greece and playwright Aristophanes' *The Birds* with its "Cloud Cuckoo Land," the perfect city in the sky.

"*Buck up!*"

BETTINA RIDDLE (1874–1957)

T HE WORD "BUCK" MAY BE IN THE RUNNING FOR THE MOST versatile of English words. We have "pass the buck," "a fast (or quick) buck," "young buck," "buck private," "mega bucks," "bucking bronco," "saw buck," "buck teeth," "buckskin," "That's why they pay you the big bucks," the invasive tree "buckthorn," and that energetic tap dance we call "the buck and wing." And then there's the advertising character "Bucky Beaver," the Milwaukee Bucks, the Ohio State Buckeyes, and President Harry Truman's "The buck stops here."

Bettina Riddle's series of "Pam" novels began in 1906 with *What Became of Pam*. There we read about Pam's interactions with her parents, her grandfather, her nurse, and her pet monkey. And there we also find, "Don't spoil it all by being weepy. Come, buck up, like a dear, and wish me joy." That is the earliest published appearance of our phrase, "buck up."

A final biographical note: after her marriage, Pennsylvanian Bettina Riddle became the Baroness von Hutten of Stolzenberg.

"Love makes the world go 'round."

HENRY ROBERT MERRILL LEVAN (1921–1998)

A FTER SERVING IN THE ARMY DURING THE SECOND WORLD War, Levan, known more popularly as Bob Merrill, settled in Hollywood to write dialogue for Columbia Pictures. He is best remembered for the novelty songs he composed as, for example, "If I Knew You Were Coming I'd Have Baked a Cake" recorded by Eileen Barton and "How Much is that Doggie in the Window?" recorded by Patti Page. His other Top-Ten hits include "Mambo Italiano," "Tina Marie," and "Make yourself Comfortable."

Merrill wrote "Love Makes the World Go 'Round" as the main theme for the 1961 Hollywood musical, *Carnival*. The song provided a hit single for singer Jane Morgan and later for a number of recording stars including The Hollies, Perry Como, and Madonna. Merrill's biggest hit, "People," was written for singer Barbra Streisand's *Funny Girl*. The movie version earned him Academy Award and Golden Globe nominations for Best Song.

And the "World Go 'Round" lyrics:

> I'm the one who's crawling on the ground,
> When you say love makes the world go 'round, yeah
> You say love makes the world go 'round…
> Don't you know I'm coming back around
> Cuz I say love makes the world go 'round, yeah
> Cuz I say love makes the world go 'round.

"Read my lips: no new taxes."

MARGARET ELLEN NOONAN (1950–)

TODAY, "PEGGY" NOONAN IS A POPULAR AUTHOR AND A columnist for the *Wall Street Journal*. Earlier in her career she served as the writer who provided the script for the acceptance speech delivered by George H.W. Bush at the 1988 Republican national convention. The speech included Bush's most memorable line about his lips:

> I'm the one who will not raise taxes. My opponent now says he'll raise them as a last resort, or a third resort. But when a politician talks like that, you know that's one resort he'll be checking into. My opponent won't rule out raising taxes. But I will. And the Congress will push me to raise taxes and I'll say no. And they'll push, and I'll say no, and they'll push again, and I'll say, to them, "Read my lips: no new taxes."

Reportedly, Noonan was given the "lips" idea by Jack Kemp, the former football great turned Republican politician. The lip-reading referred to is, of course, the method used by the deaf to understand spoken words by interpreting the movement and shape of the speaker's lips.

As president, Bush did agree to a tax increase; and when reporters asked about this turnabout, Bush pointed to his rear end and said, "Read my hips!" The tax increase contributed to Bush's defeat for a second term by Democrat Bill Clinton in 1992.

"He's hen pecked."

JAMES ROBERT GILMORE (1822–1903)

OUR CHICKENS HAVE GIVEN US QUITE A NUMBER OF CATCH phrases. There's "mother hen" (an overprotective mom or wife). We say we are "cooped up" (confined). We say the head of the house "rules the roost" (although the original was "rules the roast"). We don't approve of cowards who are "chicken hearted," "chicken livered," or just plain "chicken." A young woman is a "spring chicken." When we make a run for it, we're said to "fly the coop." We face the consequences when "the chickens have come home to roost."

James Gilmore wrote his novels of the American Civil War under the penname Edmund Kirke. In *My Southern Friends* (1863), Kirk (Gilmore) used his experiences as a cotton trader to comment on the evils of slavery in the South. There we find the first published reference to a husband being "hen pecked" by a domineering wife.

Finally we have this mordent reminder from Irish playwright George Bernard Shaw (1856–1950): "He may be henpecked: what married man is not?"

"He couldn't fight his way out of a paper bag."

OMAR NELSON BRADLEY (1893–1981)

URING WORLD WAR II, GENERAL BRADLEY SERVED AS commander of the United States ground forces from the invasion of Normandy to the end of the European war. He was the last of nine "five star" generals in the United States military. After his appointment as Army Chief of Staff in 1948, General Bradley lamented the sorry state of the army's organization, equipment, and training. As he recorded in his 1951 autobiography, *A General's Life*, "The Army of 1948 could not fight its way out of a paper bag."

This dismissive saying about fighting prowess gradually evolved into "could not *punch* his way out of a paper bag," and then "could not punch his way out of a *wet* paper bag." Eventually we leave fighting for such usages as "The team couldn't *play* its way out of a paper bag" or "My boss couldn't *manage* his way out of a paper bag," and the entirely illogical, "She couldn't *act* her way out of a paper bag."

We can't leave this subject without mentioning the numerous experiments in which a boxer attempts to punch his way out of an oversized paper bag in which he has been confined. The boxer invariably fails because the sides of the bag simply give way with his punches instead of breaking or tearing.

"The Iron Curtain."

ARTHUR MACHEN (1863–1947)

A CURTAIN SEEMS TO BE THE PERFECT SYMBOLIC representation of the idea of a threshold and of separation. The curtain that drops down to cover a theater's stage perfectly exemplifies this, as is manifest in our catchphrases: "final curtain" (death), "curtain call" (encore), "brings down the curtain" (concludes), and so on.

"The Iron Curtain" is also a reference to the theater. London theaters, among others, used curtains of metal because cloth curtains were considered an unacceptable fire hazard. British author Machen used this as a symbol of finality in his 1895 novel, *The Three Impostures*: "The door clanged behind me with the noise of thunder, and I felt that an iron curtain had fallen on the brief passage of my life." This was the first appearance of the phrase in print.

In 1924, author G.K. Chesterton wrote of an "iron curtain" in his weekly column for the *Illustrated London News*, November 29: "… that iron curtain of industrialism that has cut us off not only from our neighbor's condition, but also from our own past."

Finally, the distinction for applying "iron curtain" to the border between the territories of the Soviet Union and the West traces to Prime Minister Winston Churchill's address at Westminster College in 1946:

> From Stettin in the Baltic to Trieste in the Adriatic an iron curtain has descended across the Continent. Behind that line lie all the capitals of the ancient states of Central and Eastern Europe. Warsaw, Berlin, Prague, Vienna, Budapest, Belgrade, Bucharest and Sofia, all these famous cities and the populations around them lie in what I must call the Soviet sphere, and all are subject in one form or another,

not only to Soviet influence but to a very high and, in some cases, increasing measure of control from Moscow.

"Include me out."

SAMUEL GOLDWYN (1879–1974)

SAM GOLDWYN IS REMEMBERED TODAY ONLY BECAUSE HIS name is included in the trademark "MGM" (Metro-Goldwyn-Meyer). However, for those interested in phrases, he remains the source of innumerable laughable quotes. There's even a word for these: "Goldwynisms."

Examples: "I don't think anybody should write his autobiography until after he's dead." "A verbal contract isn't worth the paper it's written on." "In two words: Im Possible." "I may not always be right, but I'm never wrong." "Next time I send a damn fool for something, I'll go myself." "Our comedies are not to be laughed at." "We can always get more Indians from the reservoir." "Anyone who would see a psychiatrist should have his head examined."

Goldwyn deserves to be remembered for more than the funny quotations. Born in Warsaw as Schmuel Gelbfisz, he emigrated to the United States and eventually settled in Hollywood where he (as Sam Goldwyn) became filmdom's most successful movie producer. His *Arrowsmith*, (1931), *Dodsworth* (1936), *Dead End* (1937), *Wuthering Heights* (1939), *The Little Foxes* (1941), and *The Best Years of our Lives* (1948) all received the Film Academy's Best Picture nomination. His final film, *Porgy and Bess* (1959) was nominated for three Academy Oscars.

"The survival of the fittest."

HERBERT SPENCER (1820–1903)

THIS PHRASE IS NEARLY ALWAYS ATTRIBUTED TO CHARLES Darwin, the English naturalist famous for his theory of "evolution"—the concept that all biological species have common ancestors and have developed and become differentiated from one another through natural processes requiring eons of time. The source given is Darwin's 1859 treatise, *Origin of Species*, in which he explained his theory (but where, in truth, he gave it the term "natural selection").

In his revised 1869 edition, Darwin attributed "survival of the fittest" to the biologist-philosopher Spenser, who had used the phrase in his 1864 tract *The Principles of Biology*. In his new edition, Darwin endorsed Spencer's phrase as "more accurate" than "natural selection." And so, nothing could be clearer or better established than that Spenser is true source of "survival of the fittest," and yet we still insist on attributing the phrase to Darwin. Why is that?

The best answer to this question can be found in the fascinating 1992 reference work, *Nice Guys Finish Seventh*, by Ralph Keyes. The book is not a lexicon of quotes but rather of misquotes. Keyes' rules of misquotation are two: "Any quotation that can be altered will be," and "Famous quotes need famous mouths." The latter rule gives us Charles Darwin as the source of "the survival of the fittest."

"Don't be such a wimp!"

GEORGE ADE (1866–1944)

WHY DO WE SAY "HE WIMPED OUT" OR "THAT'S A WIMPY reply"? Experts tell us these wimpish words derive from "whimper"; but where "whimper" came from is anyone's guess. We're told that the word imitates the sound of someone who is whimpering, but that really does not ring true.

The most famous wimp, at least during the heyday of newspaper comic strips, was J. Wellington Wimpy who appeared with the one-eyed, pipe-smoking Popeye in the comics and in the animated cartoons created by cartoonist E.C. Segar (1894–1938). Popeye loved spinach— "I fights to the finish 'cause I eats my spinach," but Wimpy loved hamburgers even more.

Incidentally, the Wimpy cartoon character provided the name for the British chain of Wimpy hamburger restaurants.

George Ade was an American humorist, newspaper columnist, and playwright. The earliest published appearance of any phrase about wimps will be found in Ade's 1920 collection, *Hand-Made Fables*: "The next day he sought out the dejected wimp."

"*Black Magic.*"

EDMUND SPENSER (1552–1599)

LACK MAGIC IS LOVE," OR SO SAYS A BARBARA STREISAND lyric popularized by singer Ella Fitzgerald: "That old black magic has me in its spell—that old black magic that you weave so well." However, the phrase has always had, or at least since Edmund Spenser's day, another and less agreeable meaning.

Spenser, an early and highly influential English poet, finished his crowning masterpiece in 1590, his epic poem *The Faerie Queen*, which celebrated in allegory the reign of his own queen, Elizabeth I. The first published appearance of the phrase "black magic" is found in in the poem as follows:

> For he the tyrant, which her hath in ward
> By strong enchauntments and blacke Magicke leare,
> Hath in a dungeon deepe her close embard,
> And many dreadfull feends hath pointed to her gard.

A list of other popular phrases revolving around the word magic will include "magic spell," "magic carpet," "magic lantern" (the earlier name for a slide projector), "magic trick," "magic wand," "magic number" (the sum of a leading team's wins and its opponent's losses that will assure the leader of post-season or championship play), and "magic bullet" (a sought-after a cure for an intractable disease or other problem).

"Tongue in cheek."

SIR WALTER SCOTT (1771–1832)

SCOTT NO LONGER ENJOYS THE IMMENSE POPULARITY THAT once was his. During his lifetime his writings had an international following and earned him universal critical acclaim. That is no longer the case today, but there is no denying his influence on other writers: Charles Dickens, Honore Balzac, and James Fennimore Cooper, to name a few, all acknowledged their debt to Scott, especially for his historical novels such as *Ivanhoe* and *Rob Roy*.

In his 1826 novel *The Fair Maid of Perth*, Scott was first to use "tongue in cheek," the facial expression that signals that what is being said is not to be taken seriously. We can say something "with tongue in cheek," or we can say it "with a straight face."

We have a wealth of other popular phrases that revolve around the tongue: "tongue twisters," for example, and "sharp tongued," "tongue lashing," "tongue tied," "the tip of my tongue," "bite your tongue!" (or "hold your tongue!"), our "mother tongue," a "loose tongue," and many more.

Finally (couldn't resist this one) there's the poisonous evergreen shrub called "mother-in-law's tongue."

"A New York minute."

WILLIAM MILLS IVINS, JR. (1881–1961)

*H*OW LONG IS A MINUTE IN THE BIG APPLE? ACCORDING to comedian Johnny Carson, the former late-night television talk-show host, a New York minute is "the interval between a Manhattan traffic light turning green and the guy behind you honking his horn." Time flies in New York City.

The phrase first appeared in print in in 1974 when lawyer Ivins, who was at the time the curator of the art print collection at the Metropolitan Museum of Art, declared that he would vote for a given initiative without delay if certain provisions were added: "I'll vote for the Ceramics Research Center in a New York minute if I can just get initiative, referendum and recall added."

Visitors to the city often remark on the frantic pace they find in "the city that never sleeps." One Manhattanite was quoted in a blog as follows: "The morning is considered a full day, the afternoon is considered another day, and the evening is another day. So there are three days of work to be done in one day. Visitors feel the energy."

"A no-brainer."

CARL ALFRED GRUBERT, JR. (1911–1979)

*I*FIRST HEARD THIS PHRASE MANY YEARS AGO WHEN DISCUSSING events with one of the members of a board that had made an unfortunate decision. "Yes, I was disappointed at the vote," he said. "I would have thought it was a no-brainer."

This phrase, especially considering the relatively recent date for its arrival in our language, has a surprising range of meanings and applications. Its first published appearance occurred in 1950 in cartoonist Grubert's long-running newspaper comic strip, *The Berrys*. The parents, Pat and Peter Berry, are playing gin rummy together as Peter scores yet another easy win—in the vocabulary of gin, a "no-brainer" because Peter was dealt a hand that had the right cards for a fast win requiring little mental effort. Thus Pat exclaims, "Peter! Not another no-brainer!"

The meaning of "automatic" was first applied in sports, as for example, to describe the hockey or tennis player who makes a play by reacting so quickly that no decision-making process could have been involved. Then the 1980's investment advisors began applying the phrase to investments that require no active management (money-market funds, for example). A decade later, this phrase, now with the meaning of "impossible," was applied by politicians to describe self-defeating government policies. Then we find this meaning: "an activity that requires little or no thought," as, for example, a "no-brainer" college course. Finally, there's the stupid person: "The club included a group of no-brainers who wouldn't listen to reason."

"*I kid you not.*"

HERMAN WOUK (1915–)

ERMAN WAUK IS MOST REMEMBERED FOR HIS 1952 Pulitzer Prize winning novel, *The Caine Mutiny*, which related events that took place on a naval destroyer in the Pacific during World War II. Many will also remember the 1954 movie version starring Humphrey Bogart (1899–1957). Wouk's leading character, Lieutenant-Commander Queeg, used "I kid you not" several times in the novel, thus introducing the saying to the reading public. Wouk's biographers have said that he borrowed the phrase from his younger brother Victor, an electrical engineer.

For many the statement will ever be associated with Jack Paar (1918–2004), the television comedian whom critics say perfected (if not invented) the late-night comedy talk format while hosting *The Tonight Show* on NBC from 1957 to 1962. Paar rarely missed an opportunity to punctuate his assertions with "I kid you not."

The phrase later evolved into the use of a concluding "not" to contradict what had just been said (as in "I really love opera... NOT!") But the first published use of the "kid you not" affirmation must be credited to author Wouk.

'Lower the boom."

JOHN NORMAN HARRIS (1915–1964)

WE ARE ALL FAMILIAR WITH SEVERAL OF THE COMMON meanings of the word "boom." First of all, "boom" and "kaboom" imitate the sound of an explosion. We may own a "boom box." We may hear a "sonic boom." Furthermore, we understand that if something is "booming" it's growing rapidly, figuratively exploding (note "boom town," "baby boom," and "the recent boom in municipal bonds"). Still, the idea of "lowering" a "boom" doesn't seem to fit—although we all understand what happens when someone "lowers the boom" on someone else.

The mystery is easily solved when we learn that this meaning of "boom" refers to the boom of a sailboat, the long pole that that holds the bottom of the sail. The boom can represent a danger to sailors who are struck on the head when the boom is unexpectedly lowered on them. This word "boom" has nothing to do with explosive noises—it was derived from the Dutch word for "pole."

John Harris was a Canadian author whose mystery novel, *The Weird World of Wes Beattie* was published during the year of his death. There we find the first printed use of our phrase: "Wes had been borrowing from everybody and his brother and the boys lowered the boom on him."

"*Shine on, harvest moon.*"

NORA BAYES (1880–1928) AND JACK NORWORTH (1879–1959)

*T*HIS ONCE IMMENSELY POPULAR SONG WAS INTRODUCED in the Ziegfeld Follies of 1908 by the married songwriters Bayes and Norworth. Pianist George Gershwin accompanied the pair. The lyrics (in part):

> Snow time ain't no time to stay
> Outdoors and spoon;
> So shine on, shine on, harvest moon,
> For me and my gal.

But why was the moon called a "harvest" moon? That moon is the full moon that occurs closest to the autumnal equinox (when days and nights are of equal length), and farmers harvested their crops late in the evening (after sunset) by the light of that moon. Furthermore, at least in in myth and folklore, the full moon of each month is given its own name. Examples are "the wolf moon" in January, "the snow moon" in February, and "the flower moon" in May.

It must be added that Jack Norwood's song credits include "Take Me Out to the Ballgame," the perennial favorite among baseball fans, which he composed in 1908.

"Tennis anyone?"

GEORGE BERNARD SHAW (1856–1950)

THIS INVITATION WILL BE FOREVER ASSOCIATED WITH screen-actor Humphrey Bogart (1899–1957), recalled from his earlier years on the Broadway stage. However, Bogart once swore to language pundit William Safire that he never once repeated the line on stage (or anywhere else). Bogart readily admitted that he had once played a minor role dressed as a tennis player, but he was not then or ever given the "Tennis anyone?" line to recite. However, "Tennis anyone?" does appear in a theatrical play—one written by Shaw.

George Bernard Shaw was a respected Irish music and literary critic who later became Ireland's most renowned playwright. We also note in passing that he is the only person to have been awarded both the Nobel Prize for literature and filmdom's Academy Award (for penning the script for the movie version of his play *Pygmalion*). The "Tennis anyone?" line appears in his 1914 play, *Misalliance*.

The line also provided the pianist-comedian Victor Borge with one of his standard punch lines. During a routine in which he mangled everyday words by adding a number ("before" would become "be-five" and "create" would become "cre-nine," and so on). Thus Borge would deadpan, "Eleven-nis any two?"

"The Big Apple"

MILTON MESIROW (1899–1972) AND
BERNARD WOLFE (1915–1985)

QUITE A NUMBER OF OUR AMERICAN CITIES HAVE NICKNAMES readily recognizable by most of us. New Orleans is "The Big Easy." Hollywood is "Tinsel Town." San Francisco is "Frisco." Denver is "The Mile-High City." Chicago is alternately "The Second City," "Chi-Town," or "The Windy City" (although whether that is because of the Lake Michigan breezes or the City Hall politicians remains in dispute).

Indianapolis is "Naptown," Detroit is (or was) "Motor City." Saint Paul and Minneapolis are the "Twin Cities." Kansas City is "K.C." In the bad pun department we have "Lost Wages, Nevada." Cincinnati is "Cincy" and Philadelphia is "Philly" (and "The City of Brotherly Love," of course). Nashville is "Music City."

New York City requires its own list. Aside from "The Big Apple," there is "The City So Nice, They Named It Twice" (*i.e.*, New York, New York), "The City That Never Sleeps," and "Gotham."

In *Really Blues* (1946), "Mezz" Mezzrow, a blues saxophonist from Chicago, and Bernard Wolfe, a professional writer, were the first to use the nickname "Big Apple" in print: "As soon as we hit the Big Apple we'll ditch the buggy, and when the New York cops find it, your insurance company will have to ship it back to you."

"Nine days wonder."

GEORGE HERBERT (1593–1633)

*W*HY *NINE* DAYS? SOME PUNDITS BELIEVE THAT THIS number refers to newborn puppies or kittens; born blind, they gain their sight in nine days. The idea is that these newborns have no visual information to go on and can only wonder at the world around them. (I'll leave it to you readers to decide if that explanation is persuasive.)

The phrase about "nine days" is now applied to any passing fad—a headline grabbing sensation for a short time and then entirely forgotten as the next wonder takes its place on center stage. This reminds us of the music industry's "one-hit wonders." We also note that during World War II, the graduates of fast-track officer training programs were known, dismissively enough, as "ninety-day wonders." And, last, we are reminded of the nine days of the Catholic devotion called a "novena," the repetition of prayers (usually prayers of petition) each day for nine consecutive days.

The English poet George Herbert was a member of parliament until he renounced all earthly ambitions to become an Anglican parish priest. He was renowned for his saintly devotion to his parishioners. Herbert's 1633 poem "The Temple" gives us the first published instance of our phrase: "The brags of life are but a nine days wonder."

Finally, we note that Shakespeare had a close approximation of the phrase in his 1591 play, *Henry VI part 3*:

> *King:* "You'd think it strange if I should marry her."
> *Gloster:* "That would be ten days' wonder, at the least."
> *King:* "That's a day longer than a wonder lasts."

"King of the Hill."

JEAN LE BEL (1290–1370)

THIS PHRASE WILL REMIND YOU, AT LEAST IT WILL REMIND you older readers, of a children's game (for some, "king of the *mountain*" or "king of the *castle*"). The object was for one of the kids to occupy the top of a hill, mound, or pile of debris and to fight off all the others who were trying to displace him (or less often *her*) by pushing and shoving and sometimes even punching and kicking. Today, "king of the hill" can represent any competitor, adult or child, who succeeds by besting all rivals in the struggle to overthrow the reigning king of something or other. This could be in commerce, politics, show business, or grammar school stuff.

Our younger readers will more readily think of the animated comedy television series, *King of the Hill* that aired on Fox Network from 1997 to 2010.

For history buffs, "king of the hill" will take them back to the fourteenth century and the battle in which the English King Edward's much smaller forces, entrenched in a hilltop fortress, repelled the attack of King Phillipe of France. After the battle, according to the *Chronicles* of Jean le le Bel, Edward became popularly known as "the King of the hill."

"Can't hold a candle to…"

WILLIAM EDWARD NORRIS (1883–1925)

*W*E ASSOCIATE HEAT WITH AND LOVE AND AFFECTION. We say, "I have a warm spot in my heart for you," and we sing (or listen to) "torch songs" when we've been "carrying a torch for someone" who is now our "old flame." We may even admit to having a "burning desire." Furthermore, oldsters may remember, as lyricist Otto Harbach reminded us in the 1933 musical *Roberta*, that "when the lovely flame dies, smoke gets in your eyes." Somewhat younger readers may be reminded of the 1960's and the recording of "Hot Love" by Rick Nelson's Cheap Trick quartet.

Does all of this warm-hearted business explain our "candle" cliché? In a word, no. That phrase has nothing to do with romantic love; for, as the historians tell us, in bygone days while learning a trade, one task for apprentices was to provide light for the master's work by holding a candle to illuminate the workspace. We really do not measure up if we are not even worthy of that lowly job.

William Norris was a prolific English author of short stories and novels. The first published record of the phrase about holding a candle is found in his *No new Thing* (1883): "Edith is pretty, very pretty; but she can't hold a candle to Nellie."

"*Put your best foot forward.*"

SIR THOMAS OVERBURY (1581–1613)

THIS INSTRUCTION, MEANING "DO YOUR BEST," RAISES AN interesting question. Grammarians tell us that in comparing two items, one of the two might be "better," but that there is no "best" of two. Assuming we're not advising four-footed animals, why then do we say "*best* foot?" At least Shakespeare knew better. In the play *King John* (1595), in Act I, Scene 2, Shakespeare has, "Nay, but make haste, the *better* foot before." The one explanation that makes sense is that when we want to urge people to do their utmost to accomplish some task, we want to use the superlative "best" rather than the wishy-washy "better," and grammarians be hanged.

Sir Thomas Overbury was an English poet whose 1613 poem "A wife" includes "He is still setting his best foot forward." This is the first published instance of the use of the advice to use our "best foot."

We also note here that Overbury was the victim of a notorious murder. It is a complicated story, but briefly the facts are that while imprisoned in "the Tower," Overbury was poisoned with a mixture that included sulfuric acid—this was to keep him from testifying to what he knew about a plot against King James.

"Honesty is the best policy."

AESOP (620–560 BC)

THIS MAXIM COULD HARDLY BE OLDER. IT TRACES BACK TO Aesop, still famous as ancient Greece's great collector of fables. We are told he was a former slave from the region we now know as the Balkan Peninsula. His fable "Mercury and the Woodcutter" is the ultimate source for "Honesty is the best policy."

Briefly summarized, the fable tells us that the woodcutter has lost his ax in a river. The god Mercury offers him a golden ax, which the woodcutter does not accept as truly his own. Mercury then presents him with both his old ax and the gold ax as a reward for his truthfulness. We know the moral.

We might briefly stop to quibble about our translators' use of the word "policy." Dictionaries inform us that a "policy" specifies a principle of action that guides us to what is to our advantage. Students of the moral virtues might wonder at the implication that we should be honest not for honesty's sake but to gain some benefit (rather than following the adage of John Henry Newman (1801–1890) that "Virtue is its own reward." But of course, just possibly gaining an advantage is the fable's intended meaning.

"I don't have ulcers. I give them."

DAVID SARNOFF (1891–1971)

T HIS BOAST WAS BORROWED BY A LARGE NUMBER OF "ULCER givers," and each of them is often quoted as the originator of the claim. Among these, famously, are movie producer Sam Goldwyn, President Lyndon Johnson, New York Mayor Ed Koch, football coach Vince Lombardi, basketball coach Bill Fitch, and Hollywood studio head Harry Cohn. Lombardi's version was: "I don't have ulcers, I'm a carrier."

The irony inherent in the claim to "give ulcers" is that (as medical professionals inform us) those painful holes in the lining of the stomach called ulcers are not caused by stress or by spicy foods but rather by harmful bacteria (much as is the case with so many other human diseases).

Sarnoff, a Russian-born American businessman, was an early radio and television pioneer. His empire included both RCA and NBC. Was he hard to work for? Well, aside from his boast about ulcers, another clue is that his employees referred to him as "the General."

"At the end of the Day."

KELLIE COFFEY (1971–)

THIS CLICHÉ HAS BEEN CITED BY ANY NUMBER OF authorities as the "most hackneyed," "most irritating," and "most over-used," of journalism's favorite and most-repeated phrases. It is often defined by another winner, "when all is said and done…" thus compounding the linguistic felony. Other recent winners in the cliché derby have been "pearls of wisdom," "moment of truth," "it's in the bag," "one fell swoop," "call a spade a spade," "the last straw," "too much of a good thing," "let sleeping dogs lie," "going forward," "let's touch base," "thinking outside the box," and "the tail is wagging the dog." Of course the complete list would fill volumes.

The experts have been unable to track down the first writer who used "end of the day" in print, and so here I cite song-writer and country-music performer Kellie Coffrey's 2002 hit single, "At the End of the Day." The 1985 English-language musical version of Victor Hugo's *Les Miserable* also included a song with that title. And, finally, we note the 2010 independent film *War Games: At the End of the Day.*

"*The game is afoot.*"

WILLIAM SHAKESPEARE (1564–1616)

E MUST KEEP IN MIND THAT THE WORD "GAME" HAS two distinct meanings. We have the "game" that hunters pursue—quarry such as birds (pheasants, wild turkeys), fish (bass, trout), animals (rabbits, deer), and the so-called "big game animals" (lions, tigers, buffalo, elephants, and rhinos—now protected from hunters by law).

Then we have competitive games—contests with rules of play such as athletic sports (baseball), parlor games (charades), board games (Monopoly), card games (poker), gambling games (craps), children's games (hide and seek), television game shows (*The Price is Right*), and so on. We must also note that "Gaming the system" means to abuse the rules of a game to achieve an unfair advantage. This idea of gaming was brought to its logical extreme in Stephen Potter's 1947 best-selling book *Gamesmanship*, which he described as "the art of winning games without *actually* cheating."

"The game is afoot" (which means "the prey is on the move") was first used by Shakespeare, but it is most often associated with the great fictional detective Sherlock Holmes. Shakespeare: "Before the game is afoot, thou still let it slip" (*King Henry IV Part I*—1597). Sir Arthur Conan Doyle's Holmes: "Come, Watson, come! The game is afoot" ("The Adventure of Abbey Grange"—1905).

"Now I lay me down to sleep."

BENJAMIN HARRIS (1673–1716)

ERE IS A PRAYER THAT ONCE WAS GENERALLY KNOWN and regularly recited by every English-speaking Christian child. It first appeared in England in Harris' *The Protestant Tutor* and in the New World in his *New England Primer*:

> Now I lay me down to sleep,
> I pray the Lord my soul to keep,
> If I should die before I wake,
> I pray the Lord my soul to take. Amen.

The wording of the prayer provides the opportunity for a grammar lesson (sorry). My excuse is that the confusion over the verb "lay" and the verb "lie" is the single greatest source of grammatical error in our everyday speech and writing, and a number of grammarians have placed the blame for the confusion squarely on this prayer.

"Lay" takes an object: a hen lays an egg, a bricklayer lays bricks, a salesman lays pipe, and so on. Lie never takes an object: "I think I'll lie down," and, "Martha Jones lies at rest." It's the past tense of "lie" that confuses us. It is "lay" as in "Yesterday he lay in the sun too long." So the two different verbs each have a "lay" and many of us will say, "I think I'll lay down." Whoops.

"Knee-jerk reaction."

OSCAR ODD MCINTYRE (1884–1938)

THIS REACTION IS AN AUTOMATIC REFLEX OF THE KNEE tendon, technically termed (by physiologists) as the "patellar reflex" because it is caused by striking the patellar ligament in the knee. The strike sends a signal to the spinal cord, which then sends an impulse back to the leg muscles causing them to contract and the leg to kick out.

The phrase is readily applied to social situations. When we react to something said or done—without stopping to think—we are said to have had a "knee-jerk reaction." In politics, it is often applied to a new policy (or law) enacted too quickly, without proper discussion and debate. In neither case is praise intended.

O.O. McIntyre was a renowned American newspaper columnist in the nineteen-twenties and thirties. In an October 1921 column (published in more than five-hundred newspapers), he wrote: "An itinerant preacher stemming Broadway on a soap box gets only an occasional knee-jerk reaction." This was the first published instance of the metaphorical use of our "knee-jerk" catchphrase.

"It boomeranged."

JAMES BRUNTON STEPHENS (1835–1902)

W E HAVE LEARNED ABOUT SOME INTERESTING ANIMALS from our Australian friends, and many of us have made their acquaintance at the zoo—and their names: kangaroo, dingo, koala, wallaby. And those Australian words! Consider just one popular Australian song, "Waltzing Matilda." There are words in just the first stanza of those lyrics that present more of a challenge than most of us can meet: Who or what is a "swagman"? What is a "billabong"? What is that "billy" he's boiling? And of course, what is "waltzing Matilda" supposed to convey to us?

And then there's that weapon. Or is it a plaything (like a Frisbee)? Boomerangs return to those who throw them. And so we have the verb "to boomerang," which means to backfire—to have the opposite effect than that intended or to return to a previous condition. Thus the headlines: "Boomerang Patients Challenge Hospitals" and "Smartphones Boomerang from Compact to Supersized."

J.B. Stephens, a school teacher by profession, was born in Scotland but immigrated to Australia in 1866. There, in 1880, he published his one book of poetry. That is where we find the earliest printed use of our Australian word as a verb: "War shouts and universal boomeranging."

"*Speak of the Devil.*"

GIANELLO TORRIANI (1500–1585)

TODAY WHEN WE ARE DISCUSSING SOMEONE WHO THEN appears in our doorway, we say "Speak of the Devil" (or in England "*Talk* of the devil") as a warning that we must change the subject or at least avoid any negatives to which the newcomer might take offense. Or perhaps there is no warning implied at all, for the phrase might merely be the equivalent of "Look, there she is now!"

The original of the phase was much more sinister. It was a serious admonition not to speak of the devil because such talk might actually trigger the Devil's appearance! Such a dangerous encounter was to be avoided, to say the least.

The first recorded appearance of this ominous warning appears in 1566 in Torriani's *Piazza Universale* ("The Universal Square"): "The English say, 'Talk of the Devil, and he's presently at your elbow.'" Richard Trench, the Dean of Westminster in the mid nineteenth century, agreed with the prohibition and explained that "it contains a very needful warning against curiosity about evil."

"Kitty cornered."

JOSEPH CLAY NEAL (1807–1847)

When I was a lad, we said that two things situated diagonally from one another across a square were "kitty cornered" from one another (As an example, "The lot is on the northwest corner of Fifth and Main, kitty cornered from the park.") Later in life, friends corrected me: "Don't you know it's 'catty cornered,' not 'kitty cornered'?" Still others insisted we were mispronouncing "cater cornered."

What we really have here is simply an Anglicization of the French "quatre" ("four"), and thus, our catchphrase originally meant simply "four cornered." It later morphed into meaning the diagonal of a real or imaginary square.

J.C. Neal, a Philadelphia newspaper editor and humorist, published the first known mention of one of these variations of our phrase in *Charcoal Sketches or Scenes in a Metropolis*, an 1839 work of fiction. "One of that class" Neal wrote, "who, when compelled to share their bed with another, lie in that engrossing posture called 'catty-cornered.'"

"The Twist."

ASA EARL CARTER (1925–1979)

*D*O WE REMEMBER "THE TWIST"? IN THE 1960'S IT WAS a dance craze—inspired by that new kind of music we called "rock and roll." Dancers (alone, in pairs, or in groups) would plant their two feet and spin their arms and upper bodies to the music. Well, you would have to have seen it.

The twist is far from our only dance fad. In the romantic "big band" era after World War II, we danced "cheek to cheek" to slow music and we "jitterbugged" to up-tempos like "boogie-woogie." With Elvis and Rock and Roll, we rocked around the clock. Singer Chubby Checker introduced "the twist" in 1960. Then the Beatles arrived. With Vietnam, we listened to protest music by the likes of Bob Dylan. Then disco landed with the Bee Gees. And hip hop and break dancing. Then, so far as I am concerned, the dance picture becomes blurred (anybody ever dance to rap?)

Asa Carter was an American political speech writer and best-selling author (using the penname "Forrest Carter"). He was the earliest to use "the twist" in print. In a 1960 *Newsweek* article he wrote, "This heavy-beat music of the twist appeals to the base in man and brings out animalism and vulgarity." You might conclude that Carter did not approve of the twist.

"It went viral."

WILLIAM UPSKI (1972–)

ERE WE HAVE A RELATIVELY RECENT ADDITION TO OUR stock of phrases. Of course the word "viral," meaning "caused by a virus" (as in "she suffered for weeks from a viral infection") is nothing new. But "viral" meaning something that happens very quickly on the internet is fairly new. Its first appearance in print with this meaning was in 2004 in Upski's "Introduction" to his essay-collection, *How to get Stupid White Men out of Office.* There we find: "Their petition went viral, gathering half a million signatures in a few weeks."

In the bygone days before the Internet, gossip spread quickly enough by word-of-mouth. But that was nothing compared with the speed of dissemination of today's gossip (about celebrities, politics, disasters, new videos, the latest in crude sexual humor, and so on). It is simply too easy for us to forward everything and anything using our pre-existing social networks.

"Billy" Upski began as an inner-city graffiti artist, but he has now become better known as a political organizer and author.

"Low-information voters."

SAMUEL L. POPKIN (1942–)

W̲E KNOW THAT MANY OF OUR FELLOW CITIZENS VOTE in elections without studying the candidates or the questions at issue. It is true that they are less likely to get out to the polls than their better-informed cousins, but when they do vote, their choices tend to be based on comparing the physical attractiveness of the candidates or even whether they like the name of one candidate better than another's. We are also told that these voters prefer contenders who are listed higher up on the ballot. (Wily candidates know this and vie for the higher positions.)

Examples of low-information voter ("low-info" or "LIVs") preferences will include votes for candidate Bill Clinton because he likes to eat at McDonald's or votes against John Kerry because he confessed that wind-surfing is his favorite sport.

Samuel Popkin is a noted political scientist, pollster, and author who served as a consultant to the presidential campaigns of both Bill Clinton and Al Gore. The concept of the low-information voter was first discussed in print in his 1991 book, *The Reasoning Voter: Communication and Persuasion in Presidential Campaigns.* Professor Popkin's choice of words for the clueless voter was charitable: low-information voters are unpatriotic ignoramuses, and that's the truth of it.

"Hedge your bet."

GEORGE VILLEIRS, 1ST DUKE OF BUCKINGHAM (1592–1628)

W E ALL KNOW THAT A HEDGE IS A ROW OF SHRUBS planted closely together so as to form a sort of fence. Many of us will be mildly surprised, however, to learn that the verb "hedge" has basically the same meaning: "to set up a wall of protection against a loss, especially a financial loss." The so-called "hedge fund" uses strategies such as balancing short and long positions to protect the investor during both rising and falling prices. We also say someone is "hedging" when they qualify an opinion with such words as "possibly" or "at least that's what I heard."

Shakespeare, in his *Merry Wives of Windsor* (1600), was the first to use the latter meaning of "hedge" in print: "I myself sometimes, am fain to shuffle, to hedge, and to lurch."

But the use of our phrase about betting traces to Villeirs who was, among many other things, an author who cut a colorful figure at the English court during the reign of James I. Alexander Dumas put him in his novel *The Three Musketeers*, and he appeared as a character in a number of other works of historical fiction. Our phrase about "hedging" first appeared in print in Villeirs' 1672 play, *The Rehearsal*: "Now, Critics, do your worst, that here are met; for, like a rook [cheater], I have hedged my Bet."

"A slam dunk."

FRANCIS DAYLE HEARN (1916–2002)

MANY OF US HAVE DUNKED A DONUT OR BEEN DUNKED under water while swimming. Fewer of us have dunked a basketball (jumped high enough to drop the ball through the hoop rather than shoot the ball from the gym floor). Of course, slamming the ball down through the hoop with a great deal of force requires even more ability. That's the maneuver we call a "slam dunk." The phrase was coined by the legendary sportscaster "Chick" Hearn who described the play of the Los Angeles Lakers professional basketball team for radio listeners from 1965 to the year of his death.

The basketball terms originated by Hearn include "air ball," "no harm, no foul," "triple-double," "finger roll," "charity stripe," "give and go," and many more. His "slam dunk," however, is now applied in areas that have nothing to do with basketball, but rather to any sure thing: a case in point is the recent headline: "Betting on Miami: It's a Slam Dunk," that is, backing Miami is the safest bet there is, something we might call a "no brainer" —see above.

One quick historical note: A YMCA instructor named James Naismith invented the game of basketball in 1881. He nailed a peach basket up at each end of the gymnasium, divided the lads into two teams, and challenged them to toss a soccer ball into the basket defended by the other team. Needless to say, the game caught on.

"*Santa Claus.*"

HENRY WADSWORTH LONGFELLOW (1807–1882).

T HE NAME "SANTA CLAUS" WAS DERIVED FROM "SAINT Nicholas," the legendary fourth-century gift-giving bishop. The relationship between that saint and our pudgy, red-suited Christmas-gift giver is tenuous at best. The Dutch who came to the New World brought along their tradition of "Sinterklass," a jolly pipe-smoker who drove his horse-drawn wagon through the skies on Christmas Eve dropping gifts down the chimneys of those homes where deserving children lived. That figure eventually evolved into our familiar Santa.

Longfellow was a leading nineteenth-century American poet, the most popular poet of his day. His best remembered works include "Paul Revere's Ride," *The Song of Hiawatha*, and *Evangeline*. His younger brother and biographer, the Reverend Samuel Longfellow, quotes Henry as follows: "Bifana acts here [in Italy] the same comedy for children that Santa Claus does in America." That is the first published mention of that portly red-suited fellow who now holds court in our department stores during the Christmas shopping season.

The "Bifana" Longfellow was referring to is the old woman of Italian folklore who brings gifts to children during the night of January 5, the Eve of the Feast of the Epiphany (which celebrates visit of the three wise men).

"That's where the money is."

WILLIAM SUTTON (1901–1980)

THIS IS WILLIE SUTTON THE BANK ROBBER, A COLORFUL thief in the tradition of Robin Hood and Jesse James. Sutton's bank robbing career lasted forty years during which he robbed one hundred banks and stole some two million dollars. (That was real money in those days). Sutton was known for never having harmed anyone as he plied his trade (other than financially, of course). He often wore disguises and that earned him the nickname "Willie the Actor." Finally, in 1952, he was put behind bars to stay. He was a popular figure in prison because of his wit and because of the astute legal advice he readily offered.

Our interest in Sutton as a phrase-maker, traces to a reporter's question about why he had turned to crime. "So, what made you decide to rob banks?" the reporter asked. To Sutton the answer was only too obvious. His reply, "Because that's where the money is" is now as well remembered as Sutton himself.

"Bad mouthed."

JAMES GROVER THURBER (1894–1961)

*I*N HIS DAY, JAMES THURBER'S REPUTATION FOR WITTY commentary on the lives of ordinary people was unsurpassed. He is recalled today chiefly for his contributions to the *New Yorker* magazine: illustrations, cartoons, and short stories. His best remembered story is undoubtedly "The Secret Life of Walter Mitty" (1939) and the (1947) movie version starring Danny Kaye in the title role.

Mitty was a dreamer, and in his fantasies he always played the heroic role far removed from his boring and humdrum real life. And we have Thurber to thank, indirectly it is true, for the word "Mittyesque," which was coined in 1958. The word refers to all ineffectual daydreamers who remind us of that Thurber character.

And for "bad mouthed," or at least for the first published appearance of the phrase, we look to Thurber's *Saturday Evening Post* magazine article of April 9, 1941. There we find "He bad mouthed everybody." The phrase means, of course, "to disparage and to belittle."

"*A wardrobe malfunction.*"

JUSTIN RANDALL TIMBERLAKE (1981–)

THE ANNUAL SUPER BOWL FOOTBALL CHAMPIONSHIP GAME is an event like no other. First of all, it is a television show with an immense international audience. Second of all, for many viewers at least, the football contest is not the interesting thing. Some watch for the commercials. Others watch for the half-time show.

These shows have developed into ever greater extravaganzas. As to the most memorable, few will point to Michael Jackson (1996), the Blues Brothers (2002), Madonna (2012), or Beyoncé's light show in 2013 that used up all the electricity and caused a game-delaying second-half blackout. No, almost all viewers will immediately think of Janet Jackson's bared breast in in 2004.

Justin Timberlake is the big name actor and recording star who teamed with Jackson for the 2004 half-time show, and who clumsily tore open Jackson's blouse during their duet. According to Timberlake the incident was caused by a "wardrobe malfunction." Of course a "wardrobe" is a *group* of garments, and a "malfunction" is a *failure.* Timberlake was never asked to explain why he did not instead say something more like "the cause was a costume "problem" or "defect." But "Wardrobe malfunction"?

"Honey, I forgot to duck."

WILLIAM HARRISON DEMPSEY (1895–1983)

JACK DEMPSEY, "THE MAULER," CAPTURED THE IMAGINATION of the American public as an immensely popular heavyweight prize fighter in the 1920's. He held the world championship title from 1919 to 1926 during which time his fights set records for attendance and for success at the box office. However, by 1926 Dempsey had lost much of his legendary speed and punching power. He lost his championship in a bout against a younger Gene Tunney in September of that year.

In the dressing room after the fight, the bruised and battered Dempsey explained the defeat to his movie actress wife Estelle Taylor with these words: "Honey I forgot to duck." Dempsey's answer was widely reported, quoted, and remembered.

Many trace the quotation to President Ronald Reagan after the assassination attempt by the mentally deranged John Hinckley in 1981. Yes, Reagan said it. Visited in the hospital by his wife Nancy, Reagan remembered Dempsey's answer and quoted him. At the time, most Americans knew it was a quote and many knew the source.

"*Gee Whiz!*"

WILLIAM FREDERICK CODY (1846–1917)

ERE WE HAVE AN EXAMPLE OF A "MINCED OATH" (minced with the meaning of "to soften" rather than "to cut into small pieces"). "Gee whiz!"—now, more often just "gee!"— replaces "Jesus!" for those who do not want to be guilty of profaning the name of the person they take as their savior. Other familiar minced oaths are "gosh" for God, "heck" for hell, and "cripes!" for "Christ!" The origin of these phrases as oath substitutes has largely been forgotten.

"Buffalo Bill" Cody, after a notable career as a soldier and then as a buffalo hunter, is remembered today for his "Wild West" show featuring cowboys, Native Americans, and sharp shooters such as Annie Oakley. Today his memory is preserved in the popular Broadway musical (and later the film version) *Annie Get your Gun*.

The manly Cody seems an unlikely source for the first known reference to our minced oath, but his friend and long-time cast member J.V. Arlington's 1876 biography, *Life on the Border*, quotes Cody as follows: "Gee Whiz! I'll bet one hundred dollars on that hand!"

"Fairy rings."

BENJAMIN JONSON (1572–1637)

T HESE RINGS, WITHERED CIRCLES OF GRASS OFTEN SEEN on lawns and now known to be caused by fungus, were once believed to be the result of fairies dancing in a circle during the night. The first reference in literature to the rings is found in Ben Jonson's 1598 play, *Every Man in his Humour*, which was performed at the Globe Theater with actor William Shakespeare among the cast members.

Our word "fascinate" was also introduced to literature in this play. Interestingly, the word's meaning was then far removed from our definition of "to engender an intense interest in or attraction for someone" as in "He was utterly fascinated by her twinkling eyes." The meaning of the word in Jonson's day was much more challenging. It literally meant "to use witchcraft or magic to bewitch, enchant, and place under a spell." This fits, it seems to me, with the belief that rings in the grass are caused by dancing fairies in the night.

Jonson is remembered today for his satirical plays and lyric poetry. In his own time, he was renowned for his vast learning and for his influence on other dramatists and poets.

"Old geezer."

DAVID GARRICK (1717–1779)

HY IS "OLD GEEZER" A PHRASE? I AM UNABLE TO SAY why we rarely hear "geezer" without its companion word "old." The same may be said of "codger" and of "coot"— these are nearly always "old codger" and "old coot." Well, at least "graybeard" stands on its own. And then there is this from the history of the word "geezer": it derives from "guizer"—someone wearing a disguise or costume. From there we evolve the meaning of someone acting eccentrically and then finally to our eccentric old man.

Furthermore, it seems that our language finds elderly men eccentric or crotchety without supplying similar designations for elderly women. Dictionaries tell us that an "old coot" and an "old codger" are "eccentric." There are no similar descriptive words in the language for our elderly lady friends.

David Garrick was an English actor and playwright who introduced and popularized a realistic style of stage acting as opposed to the pompous and exaggerated style of delivering lines then prevalent among actors. We find the first published instance of "old geezer" in his 1775 play *Bon Ton*: "My Lord's servants call you an out-of-fashion, old geezer."

"Absence makes the heart grow fonder."

THOMAS HAYNES BAYLY (1797–1839)

"Out of sight, out of mind."

ARTHUR HUGH CLOUGH (1819–1861)

FOR GUIDANCE ALONG THE PATHS OF LIFE WE CAN LOOK to old sayings and proverbial wisdom. If we do, however, we will find more than a few contradictions. Examples?

- Look before you leap. He who hesitates is lost.

- Never put off till tomorrow what you can do today. Don't cross the bridge until you come to it.

- Many hands make light work. Too many cooks spoil the broth.

- Two heads are better than one. Paddle your own canoe.

- Haste makes waste. Time waits for no man.

- You're never too old to learn. You can't teach an old dog new tricks.

- It's better to be safe than sorry. Nothing ventured, nothing gained.

Bayly and Clough were both nineteenth-century English poets. Bayly was known for the hundreds of songs he composed. Clough is remembered more for his work with the famous nurse, Florence Nightingale. The line about "absence" is found in Bayly's poem, "Isle of Beauty." The contradictory "out of sight" appears in Clough's poem, "Of Sight."

"*The medium is the message.*"

HERBERT MARSHALL MCLUHAN (1911–1980)

Marshall McLuhan was an obscure Canadian English Professor until 1964 when he burst into public awareness with the publication of his international bestseller, *Understanding Media*. It was a survey of all human history and human knowledge. His book delighted the reading public and infuriated his academic colleagues. They began by contradicting him and then ended by ignoring him. Since then, McLuhan has largely faded from view.

McLuhan reduced everything to media. He declared that previous commentators had erred by focusing on the content of books or manuscripts or motion picture films. Instead, the truth of things, he declared, can only be revealed by forgetting about content and looking at the way a medium shapes our perceptions regardless of the message. In short, the medium *is* the message.

Probably the most notorious example of McLuhan's media effect occurred in 1960 when seventy million people watched the first televised presidential debate. Polls showed that these viewers overwhelmingly pronounced John Kennedy the winner. Those who couldn't get to a television receiver and who listened to the debate on the radio overwhelmingly awarded the victory to Richard Nixon. Both groups heard the same debate at the same time, but by way of two different communications technologies.

"Hi-yo Silver!"

FRANCIS HAMILTON STRIKER (1903–1962)

O NLY OUR VERY OLDEST READERS WILL REMEMBER THE masked western hero, the former Texas Ranger called "The Lone Ranger," his silver bullets, his powerful stallion "Silver," his faithful Native American companion, "Tonto," and their adventures as dramatized in the immensely popular radio series that began in 1933. However, those readers, few though they may be, will probably be able to recite word-for-word the breathless introduction, spoken over the opening strains of the overture to (Gioachino Rossini's opera) *William Tell*:

> Return with us now to those thrilling days of yesteryear. With his faithful Indian companion Tonto, the daring and resourceful masked rider of the plains led the fight for law and order in the early west. A fiery horse with the speed of light, a cloud of dust and a hearty "Hi-yo Silver, away!" The Lone Ranger rides again!

The show was the original conception of script-writer Striker, who also created *The Green Hornet* and *Sergeant Preston of the Yukon* for the radio. The Lone Ranger went on to even greater success as a television series starring Clayton Moore in the title role and Jay Silverheels as Tonto.

"Beethoven's Fifth."

LUDWIG VAN BEETHOVEN (1770–1827)

YOU MAY PROTEST THAT THIS IS NOT A CATCH PHRASE BUT is, rather, the name of a famous orchestral composition. And I will argue that the real name of the work referred to is "Symphony Number Five in C Minor." Adaptations in rock-and-roll, disco, and other recent musical forms have turned the words, "Beethoven's Fifth," into a pop cultural cliché. Check out "A Fifth of Beethoven" (Walter Murphy), "Roll Over, Beethoven" (Electric Light Orchestra and Chuck Berry), or "The Fifth" (Ekseption), and you will be convinced.

Beethoven is a towering figure in music history, his compositional work representing the transition from the Classical Period to the Romantic Period in serious orchestral music. Furthermore, the introductory four-note "short-short-short-long" motif (the so-called "fate motif") must be the most instantly recognizable sequence in all of music.

The "Fifth" was one of Beethoven's nine symphonies. His other works include six concertos, thirty-two sonatas, two masses, and an opera. And one more fact about Beethoven—an intensely interesting biographical fact: by 1819 he was entirely deaf and thus could neither hear his music when he composed it nor hear it in concert halls as it was rehearsed and performed.

"*Future shock.*"

ALVIN TOFFLER (1928–)

T HE JOLT DISCUSSED BY AUTHOR TOFFLER (IN HIS 1970 book *Future Shock*) refers to the psychological effect of the accelerating pace of change in our technological age. We are experiencing too much change, Toffler said, and the changes are coming at us too fast for most of us to handle. The book was an international best seller, and its influence is impossible to overestimate.

More recently, commentators David Wong and Ed Driscoll have introduced the newer phrase, "effort shock" (suggested by both "future shock" and "sticker shock") to describe the way reality slams into the lives of protected middle-class kids who have been shielded from failure in the name of promoting their self-esteem. Commentators point to the custom of not keeping score during baseball games (so that there are no losers) or of awarding all students the same score on an examination—regardless of actual performance. I confess I have no idea how prevalent these deplorable practices are, but I do know that the students involved are not being prepared for life in a world where (shockingly enough) true effort will be required of them.

"Crying wolf."

AESOP (620–564 BC)

"CRYING WOLF" HAS NOW BEEN GENERALIZED TO APPLY TO ANY situation in which we accuse someone of giving a "false alarm." The phrase comes down to us from one of Aesop's fables, "The Boy Who Cried Wolf." There we learn of a shepherd boy who amused himself by tricking the villagers into believing that his flock of sheep was being attacked by wolves. Then, of course, when a real wolf appeared, the boy's calls for help went unanswered, and his flock was scattered and destroyed. Hence the ancient-Greek philosopher Aristotle's warning that "when liars speak the truth, they are not believed."

One interesting sidelight: a recent experiment with school children indicated that after hearing the fable, the children were more, not less, likely to tell fibs. (The story about the young George Washington and the cherry tree had the opposite effect.)

We note in passing that the word "wolf" has some other interesting applications. There's the womanizer with his wolf whistle, there's wolfing down our food, and there's the "Lone Wolf" of Michael Lanyard's detective stories.

"Moving the goalposts."

NIGEL LAWSON (1932–)

Recently, journalist Bob Woodward of the *Washington Post* criticized President Obama in these words: "When the president asks for new revenue he is moving the goalposts." The phrase about goalposts was obviously borrowed from athletics—sports, which like soccer and football award points for kicking the ball accurately between upright poles defended by the other team. Moving the posts during a contest unfairly penalizes one of the teams by diminishing its ability to score (or, on the other hand, unfairly benefiting one team by making goal-scoring easier). Of course Woodward was using the phrase as a metaphor for unfairness in general or even dishonesty in general.

Baron Lawson, a journalist, Member of Parliament, and Chancellor of the Exchequer during the Thatcher administration, was the first to use "moving the goalposts" with that meaning. (Or at least that is the earliest citation reported by the authoritative British website The Phrase Finder.) In a report on a meeting of finance ministers in Kingston, Jamaica, Lawson was quoted in the daily Jamaican newspaper *The Gleamer*, as follows: "I see no reason to move the goalposts."

Lawson was created a peer for life in 1992, and he now sits in the House of Lords.

"*Every dog has his day.*"

MIGUEL DE CERVANTES (1547–1616)

HIS CLICHÉ HAS NOTHING TO DO WITH THE SULTRY "DOG days" of late summer. Those days refer to the period of time when Sirius, the Dog Star, is in ascendancy. No, this promise foretells that every dog, and thus each of us, no matter how lowly our station in life, will have a period during which we are in command. True or not, the remark has been repeated and has stayed with us since Cervantes and probably before him. It is found in the correspondence of Queen Elizabeth I (1533–1603), in 1603 in Shakespeare's *Hamlet* ("The cat will mew and the dog will have his day"), and in John Heywood's collection of maxims, *Proverbs and Epigrams*, in 1562.

Cervantes has given us a large number of our most repeated catch-phrases. Just a few examples: "Mum's the word," "Cried my eyes out," "Forgive and forget," "Not a wink of sleep," and "I smell a rat." With his *Don Quixote*, he is credited with writing the very first modern novel. Readers who have not read the book may know the work through the twentieth-century retelling of its story in the 1965 Tony-Award-winning musical play *Man of La Mancha* with its enduring theme song, "The Impossible Dream."

One last fact regarding this saying about "every dog"—in northern India, in the valleys of the Himalayas, "Dog's Day" is an annual holiday celebration in which dogs are garlanded, pampered, and fed delicacies.

"*Roaring Twenties.*"

THOMAS ALOYSIUS DORGAN (1877–1929)

W E SEEM TO HAVE FORGOTTEN ABOUT THE PERIOD IN our history that "Tad" Dorgan claimed was the decade that roared. After the devastation of the First World War and amidst the glow of peace and prosperity that replaced it, the decade of the nineteen twenties gave us jazz music, flappers (young women in short skirts with their silk hose rolled down below their knees who danced "the Charleston" far into the wee hours), hot dogs, larger-than-life movie stars and sports heroes, art deco, and new communications media (the radio, movie theaters, and the telephone).

It was a great decade for phrases, too, with "cats" signifying the admirable for some reason: "The cat's pajamas," "the cat's meow," and "the cat's whiskers." We must also not forget "the bee's knees," and "duck soup."

Dorgan was a popular American cartoonist whose phrase-making made more of a lasting impression than his cartoons. Among his many phrases: "drugstore cowboy," "for crying out loud," and the favorite nineteen twenties put down "twenty-three skidoo."

A final note: the roaring twenties came to an abrupt halt with the stock-market crash of 1929 and the ensuing "Great Depression" of the nineteen thirties.

"Achilles heel."

PUBLIUS OVIDIUS ("OVID") NASO (43 BC–18 AD)

THE ACHILLES OF THIS PHRASE IS PERHAPS THE MOST famous hero of Greek mythology. The part of his story of interest here was related by the Roman poet Ovid in his *Metamorphoses* ("Transformations"), Book 12. We learn there that shortly after his birth, his mother (the nymph Thetis) tried to make him immortal by plunging his body into the waters of the river Styx. (The Styx separates our world from Hades, the netherworld where the shades of the dead reside.) As Thetis held the infant by his heel, that heel was the one part of his body that later was vulnerable to injury. Achilles was killed when Paris, the son of the king of Troy, shot him in the heel with a poisoned arrow. We now use "Achilles heel" for the weakness in anyone's defenses, as, for example, "His ignorance of that part of the law proved to be his Achilles heel."

Homer's great epic poem *The Iliad* narrates a chapter in the Greeks' effort to recapture Helen, the most beautiful woman of Greek mythology. The narrative is largely concerned with Achilles and his refusal to fight after quarrelling with Agamemnon, the commander of the Greek forces at Troy.

Finally, we note in passing that in human anatomy, the "Achilles tendon" attaches the muscles of the calf to the heel.

"Big Brother."

ERIC ARTHUR BLAIR (1903–1950)

BLAIR WAS BORN IN INDIA OF A BRITISH FAMILY. THEY moved to England when he was a one-year-old. Writing under his familiar penname "George Orwell," Blair was surely one of the most influential authors of the twentieth century. His 1945 novella *Animal Farm* ("All are equal, but some are more equal than others") and his 1949 novel *Nineteen Eighty-Four* ("Big Brother is watching you") are still read and quoted and still have an enormous influence over our thinking. No pair of books by any other twentieth-century author sold anywhere near as many copies, and even today references to Orwell and "Big Brother" are scattered through news reports and opinion journalism.

The satire of *Animal Farm* was aimed at the dictatorship of Russia under Joseph Stalin, enforced by a brutal reign of terror. *Nineteen Eighty-Four* describes a dictatorship under which independent thinking has been made impossible through the government's rigorous control of language. The novel relates the story of Winston Smith, a bureaucrat assigned to rewriting newspaper articles of the past so that these support the current party line.

In addition to "Big Brother," Orwell also gave us "Newspeak" (language designed to make independent thinking impossible), "Doublethink" (the ability to hold two contradictory ideas at the same time), "The Thought Police" (law enforcement patrols assigned to crush dissenting opinion), "Memory hole" (for the destruction of embarrassing documents), and "Prole-feed" (media designed to control the common people's thoughts and actions). Also, Orwell is thought to have been the first to use the term "cold war" (in his 1945 essay "You and the Atom Bomb").

One final thought from author Orwell: "We have now sunk to a depth at which the restatement of the obvious is the first duty of intelligent men." (*Down and out in Paris and London,* 1933)

"*Acid test.*"

LOUIS JOSEPH VANCE (1879–1933)

T HE ORIGINAL MEANING OF "ACID TEST" TAKES US BACK TO the Gold Rush of 1849, which began at Sutter's Mill in California and expanded with three-hundred-thousand "forty-niners" who rushed to the west coast to participate in the search for gold. These miners routinely applied nitric acid to test the metals they found to identify genuine gold, and so the original meaning of the phrase was the quite literal "testing by the application of nitric acid." Figurative meanings were not long in coming as in this nineteenth-century advertising claim: "Gibson's Soap Polish has stood the acid test for over thirty years."

Louis Vance was an American novelist who earned his fame with a series of stories that traced the career of detective Michael Lanyard or "The Lone Wolf." We also note that there were eight "Lone Wolf" novels, twenty-four films, and dramatizations on both radio and television. The earliest use of our phrase for an imaginative test appears in Vance's 1923 novel, *The Destroying Angel*: "Few professional beauties could have stood, as this woman did, the acid test of that mercilessly brilliant morning."

"Acid" was also the popular name for LSD, a psychedelic drug popular in the days of the nineteen-sixty's youth protest movement known as the "counter culture." This practice gave us yet another meaning for "acid test."

"All aboard!"

OSHUA TOULMIN SMITH (1802–1877)

O CONDUCTORS STILL CRY "ALL ABOARD!" TO WARN their passengers that the final chance to get on the train is upon them? It would seem that "boarding" has more of a nautical than a cross-country flavor. The word is related to one of the older meanings of "board" as the "side" of a ship or boat. (Think of a "boarding party.") Why should anyone speak of "boarding" a train?

This minor mystery was fully explained by author Smith in his *Journal of America* (1837). There he explained that Americans, or at least their forebears, arrived in the New World by boat and brought a number of nautical terms along with them. He also pointed out that "All aboard!" was used on American riverboats before it was used as a warning to train passengers.

Aside from his writing, J.T. Smith was also known as a highly regarded Baptist preacher who served as a Captain in the Home Guard during the American Civil War.

"A-O.K."

JOHN ANTHONY POWERS (1922–1979)

*J*OHN "SHORTY" POWERS WAS PUBLIC AFFAIRS OFFICER FOR THE National Aeronautic and Space Administration (NASA) from 1959 to 1963. A highly decorated pilot who served during World War II and the Korean War, Colonel Powers was known at NASA as "the voice of the astronauts" for his ongoing commentary on the agency's space missions. When, during an early sub-orbital flight, astronaut Alan Shepherd radioed that everything was "Okay," Powers thought he had said "A-O.K." and reported that version to the press. The mistake proved impossible to correct. "A-O.K." quickly became accepted in everyday speech with the meaning of "much better than just plain O.K."

But where did we get this word "O.K." (or "okay")? We have to reach back in history to the American presidential campaign of 1840. Candidate Martin Van Buren, born in Kinderhook, New York, was given the derogatory nickname "Old Kinderhook" by his opponent William Henry Harrison. But a group of Van Buren's supporters in New York formed an "O.K. Club," and "O.K." became the rallying cry for the democrats.

Van Buren lost the election, but "O.K." quickly became the best known of all Americanisms. In fact, the American critic H.L. Mencken (1880–1956) believed that "O.K." was "the most shining and successful Americanism ever invented."

"Blows hot and cold."

AESOP (620–564 BC)

THIS PHRASE TAKES US BACK ONCE AGAIN TO OUR legendary collector of fables, Aesop of ancient Greece. Fables, of course, are very short tales ending with a moral or lesson to be learned. Here, in full, is the fable in question, "The Satyr and the Traveler":

> A man and a satyr once poured out libations together in token of a bond of alliance being formed between them. One very cold wintry day, as they talked together, the man put his fingers to his mouth and blew on them. On the satyr inquiring the reason of this, he told him that he did it to warm his hands, they were so cold. Later on in the day they sat down to eat, the food prepared being quite scalding. The man raised one of the dishes a little towards his mouth and blew in it. On the satyr again inquiring the reason of this, he said that he did it to cool the meat, it was so hot. "I can no longer consider you as a friend," said the Satyr, "a fellow who with the same breath blows hot and cold."

> The moral: "A mouth is untrue that blows both hot and cold."

We use that moral today to criticize someone (almost always a man, for some reason) who keeps changing his mind about or his emotional reaction to a plan or a relationship.

"The whole shebang."

WALTER WHITMAN (1819–1892)

*W*ALT WHITMAN WAS ONE OF THE LEADING AMERICAN poets of the nineteenth century. He is remembered today for introducing "free verse" (verse without rhyme or meter) to the American reading public with his popular volume, *Leaves of Grass* (1855), a book he continued to revise and enlarge until his death. Whitman also served as a volunteer nurse during the Civil War, and in recounting those experiences (in his 1892 *Specimen Days*) he was the first writer to use "the whole shebang," (meaning "everything"). His "shebang" meant "an enclosure.") Author Mark Twain had used "shebang" for "a vehicle" (in *Roughing It*, 1872).

Other quotable ways of saying "everything" include "the whole ball of wax," "the whole nine yards" (for the nine-cubic-yard capacity of a dump truck), "the whole shootin' match," "the whole kit and caboodle" (from two Dutch words for "package"), "everything but the kitchen sink," "everything from soup to nuts," "an arm and a leg," and "the whole enchilada." (Enchilada? That is the Mexican treat consisting of a tortilla shell stuffed with meat and covered with a spicy sauce.)

Finally, just one quote from the highly quotable Whitman: "I no doubt deserved my enemies, but I don't believe I deserved my friends." (Quoted by John Hay in a letter dated July 22, 1888)

"The Oscar."

MARGARET HERRICK (1902–1976)

HE MOTION PICTURE ACADEMY'S BRONZE STATUETTE WAS designed by the Dublin-born art director Austin Gibbons (1893–1960), and it was first presented during the 1927 award ceremonies. The trophies, which are ten inches tall and weigh about seven pounds, were at the time referred to simply as "the Academy's statuettes." The nickname was the result of an offhand comment picked up by a newspaper reporter.

Margaret Herrick served as the Academy of Motion Picture Arts and Sciences librarian until she was promoted to the position of Director in 1943. The Academy's extensive Beverly Hills library of films and related materials is named "The Margaret Herrick Library" in her honor.

It was in 1931 that Herrick was first shown the trophy. "Why," she declared, "he looks just like my Uncle Oscar." (Her uncle, a wealthy Texan named Oscar Pierce, had by that time retired to California and lived nearby.) The newspaper reporter who overheard the comment informed his readers that "Employees of the Academy have affectionately named their famous statuette Oscar." The trophy has been "the Oscar" ever since.

"Ouija board."

ELIJAH JEFFERSON BOND (1847–1921)

BOND WAS AN AMERICAN LAWYER AND INVENTOR WHO patented the "Ouija board" in 1880. This was a two-piece item consisting of a wooden board with the alphabet printed on it, and a "planchette" (a tiny three-legged triangular table). Users of the board were told to place the fingers of one hand lightly on the planchette, and then supernatural (or paranormal) forces would move the planchette from letter to letter to spell out a message. Bond partnered with businessman Charles Kennard and Kennard's employee William Fuld to market the board as a novelty product. Their Ouija Board became unbelievably popular before our world was taken over by electronic gadgets. In 1966 the business was sold to Parker Brothers, which in turn sold it to Hasbro in 1991.

But our interest here is in "Ouija board" as a phrase. Kennard had claimed that he had been given the name while using the board, and that the movements of the planchette had spelled out the word "O-u-i-j-a" for him. He claimed the word was from the ancient Egyptian, and that it meant "Good luck." When Fuld took over operations, he kept the name, but he explained more simply that it was a combination of two words meaning "yes"—the French "*Oui*" and the German "*Ja.*"

We must also mention that some mainstream religions associated the use of the Ouija board with demonic influences, and some prohibited their followers from using the device.

"Outta sight!"

STEPHEN CRANE (1871–1900)

*A*S UNLIKELY AS IT SEEMS, "OUTTA SIGHT!" PREDATES THE "hippy" movement by more than sixty years. Crane, a popular nineteenth-century American author, used the phrase twice in his 1896 novel, *Maggie, a Girl of the Streets*. Here are the quotes: (Chapter 6): "Say, Mag, I'm stuck on yer shape. It's outta sight." (Chapter 18): "You're the kind of a man we like, Pete. You're outta sight!"

The hippie counter-cultural youth movement of the nineteen-sixties is remembered today primarily for the music festival held in Woodstock, New York, in 1969—and for its own language. Many hippy words and phrases are still in use, or at least still understood: "It's a gas." (It's fun). "Go ape." (Get furious). "It's a blast." (It's lots of fun). "Boss." (Great). "Bread" (Money). "Bug out." (Depart). "I'm hip." (I'm informed.") "I'm bummed." (I'm depressed). "Right on." (Correct). "Far out." (Strange). "Cool." (Good). "Copasetic." (Very good). "Groovy." (Very, very good). "Crash." (Go to sleep). "Dig." (Appreciate). "Don't sweat it." (Don't worry)."Flick." (Movie). "A flower child." (A hippy). "The fuzz." (The police). "Slip me some skin." (Shake hands). "Hang Loose." (Relax). "Pad." (Dwelling). "Pig Out." (Over eat). "Rap session." (Discussion). "Scarf." (Eat fast). "Square." (A non-hippie). "Threads." (Clothes). "Wigging out." (Going crazy). "..you know.." (..um..) "..like.." (..er, ah, um …) "Outta sight!" (Splendid!)

And last, these two hippie declarations: "Don't trust anyone over thirty" and "We are the people our parents warned us against."

"*Practice what you preach.*"

ROWLAND HOWARD (1825–1895)

*M*ANY READERS WILL PROTEST THAT IT WAS NOT someone named Bailey who wrote this, but rather Saint Matthew, author of the first book of the Biblical New Testament. But literal translations of Matthew gave us something different:

> "According to their works do ye not; for they say and do not."
>
> "Do not act according to their works, for they talk but do nothing."

It was not until 1876 that song-writer Howard came up with "You Never Miss the Water Till the Well Runs Dry," a song with lyrics that were packed with age-old precepts like "Strike while the iron is hot." That is where we find the first published mention of our dictum:

> Waste not, want not is a maxim I would teach.
>
> Let your watch word be dispatch and practice what you preach.

Later translations of Matthew, beginning with *The Revised Standard* in 1901 ("Do not do as they do, for they preach but do not practice.") included the key words of Howard's phrase.

Last, we have this from the American commentator Charles Murray: "It would help if our elites would preach what they practice."

"Dunce cap."

CHARLES DICKENS (1812–1870)

ONCE AGAIN, DICKENS IS OUR SOURCE FOR A FIRST PUBLISHED reference. In his 1840 novel, *The Old Curiosity Shop*, Chapter 24, we find a description of a classroom that includes this: "Displayed on hooks upon the wall in all their terrors, were the cane and ruler; and near them, on a small shelf of its own, the dunce's cap, made of old newspapers and decorated with glaring wafers of the largest size." Well, education has certainly changed. No more are we likely to hear of a teacher rapping a naughty boy's knuckles with a ruler, flogging his behind with a cane, or making him stand in a corner wearing this shameful cap.

But what is or was a "dunce"? The irony is that the word derives from one of history's most brilliant scholars, the philosopher and theologian Duns Scotus (1266–1308). Those who disagreed with his teachings derided his followers as foolish "dunsmen," then "dunses" and finally "dunces."

In more recent times, our own dunces were more often penalized for misbehavior or clowning than for ignorance or stupidity. Their punishment was to be forced to stand in silence and shame in a corner of the classroom for perhaps a half-hour while wearing the cap—a large up-side-down cone made of white paper.

"*March madness.*"

HENRY VAN ARSDALE PORTER (1891–1975)

T HE NATURALISTS AMONG US WILL EXPLAIN THAT THE hare (or rabbit) is a different animal in the springtime— during its mating season. Then the nocturnal hare is seen in broad daylight, frantically chasing about in our fields and meadows. This gave us the saying, "mad as a March hare."

H.V. Porter's "March madness" has nothing to do with rabbits. While an official with the Illinois High School Association, Porter was the first to apply the term to the sport of basketball when he published an essay with that title in 1939. At the time, Porter was referring to high-school basketball post-season play. It was CBS sportscaster Brent Musburger, during his broadcasts in the early nineteen-eighties, who first used "March madness" to label the college basketball play-offs. The tournament, which features the top sixty-eight teams in the nation, is immensely popular among the millions of Americans who dutifully make their predictions and fill out their "brackets" (diagrams illustrating the pairing of opponents in the tournament) and predict the winners for each of the sixty-seven games. The amount of money wagered on these games is beyond calculation.

The tournament has also been called "the big dance," and has given us "Cinderella teams" (underdogs with surprising wins), "the Elite Eight" (last eight teams remaining), and "the Final Four" (teams playing in the two semi-final games).

"*Double whammy.*"

ALFRED GERALD CAPLIN (1909–1979)

*I*F YOU "PUT THE WHAMMY ON" SOMEONE, YOU ARE, LITERALLY or figuratively, subduing them with a hex or supernatural spell. The "double whammy" is a much more powerful attack. As proof of this, we have the testimony of Evil-Eye Fleegle who claimed that with just one of his two eyes he could "putrefy citizens to the spot." However, he admitted, he hoped he would never have to use the double whammy, "the full power of both eyes."

You will find this testimony in the archives of Al Capp's satirical *Li'l Abner* comic strip, an extremely popular and influential comic-page institution from its introduction in 1934 until just before Capp's death. Hillbilly Abner Yokum, the hero of the strip, lived in the village of Dogpatch Kentucky along with Mammy and Pappy Yokum, Salomey (the family's pet pig), and (for the love interest) Daisy Mae. Older readers will remember fondly Sadie Hawkins Day, when girls, not boys, were permitted to take the romantic initiative, and the Shmoo, a small shapeless something-or-other that could become whatever was needed to fulfill man's material wants.

Capp won numerous awards for the strip, and since his death in 1979 three biographies have appeared. *Li'l Abner* has been the subject of over forty books, and the published reprints of the strip fill twenty volumes.

"Damage control."

EDWARD LOUIS BERNAYS (1891–1995)

THE MEANING OF THIS PHRASE HERE IS NOT MEANT TO refer to physical damage that must be contained as for example at sea where damage-control teams repair below surface ruptures from grounding or hard landings, or damage from bombs and other explosives. The meaning intended here is the manipulation of news stories that might damage the reputation of a person, business, or governmental department.

Edward Bernays has been called "the father of spin" for his pioneering work in helping American tobacco and liquor manufacturers improve their reputations with the public during the first half of the twentieth century. His success was based on techniques that included the publication of facts that would favor his clients (and the suppression of facts that would injure them), phrasing the truth in the most positive way possible, careful choice of timing of announcements for maximum (or minimum) impact, and so on. Today's businesses and political operations all maintain public-relations departments as a necessary expense, and it must also be said that outright falsehoods are be included among the tools that today's "spin doctors" employ.

A final historical note: Bernays' uncle was none other than the Austrian pioneer of psychoanalysis, Sigmund Freud. Bernays used many of his uncle's theories of human behavior in formulating his own P.R. techniques.

"Pulling up stakes."

SAMUEL SEWALL (1652–1730)

HIS PHRASE SUGGESTS SOMETHING MORE PROFOUND THAN merely changing an address. It suggests a complete severance from the past, perhaps moving to a new job and relocating in a new city.

The meaning makes sense when we consider this bit of history: the earliest British settlers in America, in Jamestown and Plymouth, erected palisades (tall and strong wooden fences constructed out of wooden poles with pointed tops) to mark off the boundaries of their own properties and also of entire communities (to afford them a wall of defense in case of an attack by Native Americans). Gathering and preparing the required timber was a major effort, and so rather than repeat the entire process, the colonists who were moving would retrieve the poles and haul them to the new location. Soon, "to pull up stakes" became synonymous with relocating.

Colonist Sewell was a businessman as well as Chief Justice of the Massachusetts High Court. His published *Diary* (1674–1729) is the main source for our knowledge of the infamous Salem Witch Trials. It is also the very earliest printed record of our phrase, with this sentence: "I went to my boundaries and ordered him to pull up the stakes."

Our interest in the expression was considerably increased when we discovered that it was the very first memorable phrase to be coined in America. We learned this fact from the authoritative English website "The Phrase Finder" (http:www.phrases.org.uk).

"Spring forward, fall back."

WALTER WINCHELL (1897–1972)

"SHE FOLLOWS WINCHELL AND READS EVERY LINE"—FROM "The Lady is a Tramp," the 1937 hit song by Richard Rodgers and Lorenz Hart.

But fame is fleeting. We have forgotten the inestimable Walter Winchell, the journalist who raised gossip to the level of an art form. His *On Broadway* column for the *New York Daily Mirror* was followed by fifty million readers daily. His ABC Sunday-night radio show was a must for more listeners than those tuning in to the top-rated comedy programs (such as the Fred Allen Show or the Jack Benny Hour). Winchell's broadcasting career, wedded as it was to radio, ended with the rise of television in the nineteen fifties.

Daylight saving time, the practice of advancing our timepieces one hour during the summer to give the evenings (after work) more daylight for recreation and other activities, was instituted in the United States during World War I to reduce our use of incandescent lighting. But how is Walter Winchell related to "Daylight Savings Time"? It is simply because he made it easier to remember how to adjust to the time changes when in 1957 he popularized the exceedingly memorable line, "spring forward, fall back."

"A Pyrrhic victory."

KING PYRRHUS OF EPIRUS (318–272 BC)

*W*E SHOULD REGRET THE LOSS TO CONTEMPORARY commentary of the highly useful concept of a "Pyrrhic victory"—a triumph that so depletes one's resources that defeat in the next battle is assured.

According to the account given by the Roman historian Plutarch (46–120 AD), Pyrrhus, one of Rome's strongest opponents, defeated the Roman armies twice in battles for possession of the Greek island Irakleia during what historians call the "Pyrrhic War." During the Battles of Heraclea and Asculum, the Romans lost many more soldiers than did the Greeks, but the Romans had seemingly inexhaustible reinforcements at their disposal. This led to King Pyrrhus famous remark that "One more such victory will utterly undo us" (or, by some accounts, "If we are victorious in one more battle with the Romans, we shall be utterly ruined").

We read almost daily of some victory in politics or business that ends up costing more than it was worth. Furthermore, everyone knows firsthand of pyrrhic victories on the job and in our own circle of family and friends. For instance, Charlie knew that the departure of Jones had left a desirable corner office vacant, and so he quickly moved in. This caused such resentment among his fellow workers (who knew Charlie did not deserve this perk) that Charlie had no choice but to start looking for a new job. None of those involved, however, used the occasion to mention King Pyrrhus.

"Four flusher."

BERTHA MUZZY SINCLAIR (1871–1940)

*A*S MOST READERS ALREADY KNOW, POKER IS NOT ONE BUT several closely-related card games. These have in common: betting by contributing to a pot, five cards in the final "hand," winners determined at the end of the deal by the value of the combination of cards held and by a hierarchy among these combinations. In this system, a "flush" (all five cards of the same suit) is bested only by a "full house" (a pair plus three of a kind) and by "four of a kind."

The "flush" was named for the flush of color in our faces from exertion or embarrassment. But we note that all five cards must share that same suit. The temptation, for a low breed of cheater, is to try to pass off as a flush a hand of five red cards or five black cards in which just four of the cards are of the same suit. Such cheaters are known as "four flushers."

The phrase first appeared in print in an early story ("Phantom Herd," 1905), by author Sinclair (using her penname B.M. Bower). On page 30 we find: "Some of the four flushers kept eyeing the bluff."

A final note: the western folk hero and gun-slinger Wild Bill Hickcok was holding a two-pair poker hand when he was shot in the back. Since then, "Aces and eights" has been known as "the dead man's hand."

"*Chump change.*"

LEE EARLE ELLROY (1948–)

THERE ARE AND HAVE BEEN MANY PHRASES THAT MEAN A small amount of money. These include "pocket money," "pocket change" (and its opposite "pocket broke"), "short money," "spare change" [or] "loose change (and even) "small change," "walking around money," "pin money," and the list goes on.

But what is a "chump"? A "chump" is a fool; and, as etymologists inform us, the word derives from a blend of "chunk" and "lump." We note that those two words also blend to "lunk." Well, there are "lunk-heads" among us.

James Ellroy, a school dropout, is an American crime-fiction author known for the use in his stories of the most brutal street language. His third, fourth, and fifth novels featured police officer Lloyd Hopkins, and it is in the second of these (*The Big Nowhere*, 1988) that we find the first published use of our phrase: "Coleman knew he needed money to finance his killing spree, and he was only making chump change gigging on Central Avenue."

"Gigging"? Well a "gig" is a job, usually a temporary job, and "gigging" is seeking and then working at such a job.

"Kilroy was here."

JAMES J. KILROY (1902–1962)

*I*T BEGAN AS AN IN-JOKE IN THE AMERICAN MILITARY, progressed to an international graffiti craze, and has now become an almost entirely forgotten piece of trivia. During World War II, the "Kilroy" slogan, and the simple line drawing of a fence with a big-nosed man peering over it, was found waiting everywhere for the American invaders and most memorably on signs posted on beachheads to greet the first wave of assault troops. Before the war's end, "Kilroy" had been seen at every stop along the paths to Berlin and Tokyo.

The story of origin of the "Kilroy" slogan is fairly straightforward. During the war, J.J. Kilroy was employed as a work monitor at the Fore River shipyard where troop transports were being built. Kilroy checked the work of riveters and signed each riveter's final rivet with his name in chalk (the riveters were paid according to the number of rivets completed). Ordinarily, these signatures would have been painted over, but in the wartime rush the painting was often skipped. Thousands of troops discovered the Kilroy signatures in inaccessible places on these ships—inside sealed hull spaces, for example. To these men, this Kilroy fellow had somehow gotten there first. So to further the legend (or joke) they began placing the name and the slogan "Kilroy was here" everywhere they went.

In 1946, a shipbuilders' union held a contest to determine who the original Kilroy was. Based on the testimony of shipyard workers, including a number of riveters, James J. Kilroy was declared the winner.

"*Chit chat.*"

PIERCE EGAN (1772–1849)

S OMETHING IN OUR ENGLISH LANGUAGE LOVES ALLITERATION and the near-rhyme of phrases like "chit chat." Any number of examples come readily to mind: "sing song," "see saw," "ding dong," "bing bang," "ping pong," "zig zag" (see above), "knick knacks," "mish mash," "click clack," "hip hop," "heebie jeebies," and "tick tock."

"Chit chat" for small talk is a sort of doubling of "chat," and "chat," a shortened form of "chatter."

Pierce Egan was an early (or perhaps the very first) newspaper sports reporter. (Of course, in those bygone days, "sports" in England meant either boxing or horse racing.) The first published appearance of our phrase is to be found in Egan's *Life in London* (1821): "She rode around the circle to *chit chat* and nod to her friends."

"Ferris wheel."

GEORGE WASHINGTON GALE FERRIS, JR. (1859–1896)

YOU MAY HAVE ASSUMED THAT THE "FERRIS" REFERENCED here refers somehow to iron and thus to those entertaining rides that were constructed out of iron. Well, the name has nothing to do with the materials involved. History informs us that the very first Ferris wheel was the invention of an American structural engineer named Ferris.

The story is this: the wonder of the Paris World's Fair of 1889 was the construction of the Eiffel Tower. Visitors could ride an elevator to the top of the structure and from there enjoy a view of all of Paris. The directors of the next World's Fair, the Columbian Exposition planned for 1893 in Chicago, were hoping for something that would equal or even surpass the Eiffel Tower. George Ferris responded to the challenge with plans for a gigantic rotating wheel that would carry seated passengers up and around and at the highest point would overlook all of the fairgrounds and beyond. The directors did not believe such a contraption could possibly be safe. After Ferris obtained the endorsements of a number of respected engineers, however, the directors approved the project.

The first Ferris wheel was two-hundred sixty-four feet tall and carried thirty-six cars, each able to accommodate up to sixty passengers. Of course the wheel was a smashing success, and it spawned the uncountable number of imitation Ferris wheels to be enjoyed at amusement parks and travelling carnivals the world over.

"A nothing burger."

LOUELLA PARSONS (1881–1972)

*A*N IDEA WITHOUT MERIT, A PERSON OF NO SIGNIFICANCE (at least in the commentator's opinion), or anything seen as a dud, insignificant, or unsuccessful can be called a "nothing burger." It has often been described as "a hamburger without the burger." The phrase is especially apt for persons or things that fail to measure up to our expectations. I personally believe it is one of our funniest catchphrases.

The phrase was a favorite of journalist Louella Parsons, the writer who originated the Hollywood gossip column. Her popular articles were syndicated in four hundred newspapers, and her weekly radio show audience numbered in the millions. Parsons' specialties included Hollywood scoops, the revelation of celebrity secrets, and the reporting of juicy scandals. She remained unchallenged in this arena until rival columnist Hedda Hopper came on the scene. The two feuded endlessly.

In 1944, Parsons penned her bestselling memoir, *The Gay Illiterate*. Finally, in 1965, Parsons' column was taken over by her long-time assistant Dorothy Manners Haskell (1903–1998) who went on to fame as the inestimable "Miss Manners."

"Don't put all your eggs in one basket."

MIGUEL DE CERVANTES (1547–1616)

E RETURN TO CERVANTES' MONUMENTAL CLASSIC *Don Quixote* for the source of yet another timeless maxim. In Volume I (1605) we find this: "Tis part of a wise man to keep himself today for tomorrow, and not venture all his eggs in one basket." American novelist Mark Twain thought otherwise, however. In his novel *Pudd'nhead Wilson* (1894) we find: "Put all your eggs in one basket and watch that basket!"

There are many other egg phrases and sayings in common use: "Walk on eggs" (be very careful), "Has egg on his face" (is embarrassed), "Egging on" (encouraging or provoking someone), "Laid an egg" (flopped or failed), "A bad egg" (a villain or rogue), "Which came first, the chicken or the egg?" (a very old folk riddle), "Easter egg" (a painted chicken egg celebrating the Easter season and the arrival of Spring), and "Eggshell blonde" (Australian slang for a bald man).

And last, we note that 1945 saw the publication of *The Egg and I*, the best-selling memoir by American author Betty MacDonald, which related her experiences as the operator of a small chicken farm in Washington State.

"Hairbreadth escape."

WILLIAM SHAKESPEARE (1564–1616)

WHEN THE TRAIL GROWS COLD IN THE HUNT FOR THE source of a phrase, the wise researcher will turn to Shakespeare. Sure enough, in *Othello* (1603), Act I, Scene 3, we find this speech by Othello:

> Wherein I spake of most disastrous chances,
> Of moving accidents by flood and field
> Of hair-breadth scapes i' the imminent deadly breach,
> Of being taken by the insolent foe
> And sold to slavery, of my redemption thence
> And portance in my travels' history.

That is the first known published appearance of our phrase.

To escape by the width of a hair would seem the closest of close calls. We also say "safe by a whisker," "a close shave" (or "close squeeze"), "a squeaker," "a near miss," and "a white knuckler."

"*Deep doo-doo.*"

GEORGE HERBERT WALKER BUSH (1924–)

D O SERIOUS ADULTS—EVEN SERIOUS JOURNALISTS and politicians—use "baby talk"? Yes they do. For better or worse, we adults have no hesitation in saying that something forbidden is a "no-no," that a minor wound is an "owie" or a "boo-boo," that something very small is "itsy-bitsy," that we have "dibs" on something we want to claim, we react to good news with "goody goody," or that a spoil sport is a "party pooper."

Did you just say that something was "yucky" or that it was "yummy"? Did you say "night-night" (or "nighty night") instead of "good night"? "Upsy-daisy"? "Whoops"? Do you wear "jammies" to bed?

In 1988 George H. W. Bush was running for president after spending eight years as Ronald Reagan's Vice President. Bush (now more often referred to as "Bush Senior") was running against Democrat Michael Dukakis. After looking at opinion polls, Bush decided his prospects were precarious. His campaign, he said at the time, was "in deep doo-doo."

That and "read my lips" (see above) are, for better or for worse, the most memorable quotes from the presidency of George H.W. Bush.

"Hello girl."

MARK TWAIN (1835–1910)

HOW MIGHT ONE EXPLAIN TO THE YOUNGER GENERATION that we once lived in a world without telephones? The first telephone was patented by inventor Alexander Graham Bell in 1876. In ten short years over one-hundred fifty-thousand homes and businesses were equipped with the invention. Of course the first phones had to be connected together by land lines—at that time, orbiting communications satellites could not even have been imagined. And thus a number of homes had to share a single line. Yes, neighbors had to take their turns, and of course they could listen in on one's private conversations. They often did.

Calls were placed through telephone "operators" who worked "switchboards"—arrays of connections and plugs that permitted two callers to be connected. "Hello" became the popular way of answering the telephone. (Surprisingly enough, the word "hello" had not been in everyday use previous to this.) Thus, predictably, the telephone operators became known as "Hello girls."

The first appearance of our phrase in print was in Twain's 1889 novel, *A Connecticut Yankee in King Arthur's Court*. Here Twain's "Yankee" voices his complaint about the lack of common courtesy at court:

> "The humblest hello-girl along ten thousand miles of wire could teach gentleness, patience, modesty, manners, to the highest duchess in Arthur's land."
>
> "Hello-girl?"
>
> "Yes, but don't you ask me to explain; it's a new kind of a girl; they don't have them here."

These days, our larger businesses have operators but they are not "Hello girls." The typical response is something like, "Acme Corporation. How may I direct your call?"

"Hit the nail on the head."

JOHN STANBRIDGE (1463–1530)

FOR THOSE FEW READERS WHO HAVE NEVER DRIVEN A nail, we note (in perhaps too elementary a fashion) that the whole point of hammering a nail is for the worker to hit the nail-head end of this item with the hammer so as to drive the other end, the pointed end, into the wood. This action has given rise to a large number of popular phrases. We say a basketball player "nailed his shot from the corner." Sally boasts that she "nailed her final exam." We report that the police "nailed the suspect" after stolen goods were found in his car, but we also report that sometimes the evidence is not so easy to "nail down." A tough guy is "hard as nails." An accurate answer is "right on the nail." And you are very dead if you are "dead as a door-nail."

John Stanbridge was an English schoolmaster with a reputation as a grammarian. He became the headmaster of Magdalen College in 1488, and he is famously remembered for once having described Sir Thomas Moore as "a man for all seasons." His book on common grammatical errors, *Vulgaria* (1520), gave us the first published appearance of "He hit the nail on the head," although he is not thought to have originated the saying.

We conclude this discussion with a version of our quote (by some now anonymous joker) that turns the matter upside-down: "He hit the nail right on the thumb."

"In one ear and out the other."

JEAN RENART (1199–1250)

ERE IS ONE OF OUR VERY OLDEST CLICHÉS, A COMPLAINT that perhaps every instructor, preacher, trainer, and lecturer has had occasion to voice. It is a kind of virtual or willful deafness that we complain of.

We complain when there is a "dialogue of the deaf" (from the French *dialogue de sourds*) or when someone "turns a deaf ear" to us. And history tells us that it was famously said of the deposed King Edward of England (1284–1387) that he was "deaf to all warnings" until it was too late and the throne was lost to him.

Jean Renaut was a Norman troubadour, or, in other words, a French composer and performer of lyric poetry during the Middle Ages. His *Romance of the Rose* (*Roman de la Rose*) is perhaps the best known and certainly one of the lengthiest examples of courtly poetry. There we find the earliest known example of our phrase. Renart's wording: "Out at one ear and in at the other."

"*Monkey see, monkey do.*"

ESPHYR SLOBODKINA (1908–2002)

E SHOULD NOT BE SURPRISED THAT THIS POPULAR saying has its origins in West African Mali, a land where monkeys are a familiar part of native wildlife. The saying means that something has been learned through simple imitation but without any understanding of the thing that has been learned or what results to expect. We apply it to anyone—but more often to a child—who blindly mimics another without concern for appropriateness or consequences. (We may say instead that one person "apes" another.)

Esphyr Slobodina was a popular author and illustrator of children's books. Our "monkey" saying finds its first published appearance in her 1940 *Caps for Sale*, a retelling of African folktales.

We also note that song-writer Michael Franks used the saying in the title and lyric of his 1976 hit "Monkey See—Monkey Do." ("Love is monkey see and monkey do—would I lie to you?")

And here are some other popular monkey phrases: There is "monkeying around" and "monkey business." Men put on "monkey suits" (formal wear). Someone might "make a monkey out of" one of us. We play on the "monkey bars." An addict has "a monkey on his back." Those who are handy may use a "monkey wrench." However, the tool was actually named for its inventor Charles Moncky who patented this kind of wrench in 1858.

"We'll be there with bells on."

HENRY LOUIS MENCKEN (1880–1956)

*I*N THE UNITED STATES, AS IN THE MAJORITY OF COUNTRIES and territories of the world, road and street traffic is required by law to use the right-hand lanes. The reason the USA differs from Britain in this regard takes us all the way back to pioneer days and the large, heavy Conestoga wagons (also called "covered wagons" and "prairie schooners") that carried settlers and their belongings across the country. The best position for the drivers of these horse-drawn wagons was on the left, and so they would be closest to the center of the roadway or trail when they chose to drive down the right-hand side. Other, smaller vehicles found it easiest to follow the ruts left by the heavier wagons. This eventually led to our right-hand lane laws.

Today we take our automobile horns for granted, but the Conestogas were equipped with brass bells for signaling, and these were rung enthusiastically when the destinations were reached. That gave us our still popular "bells on" greeting. The wagons, by the way, were named for the Conestoga Valley in Pennsylvania where they were made. Furthermore, the habit of wagon drivers who rolled their own cigars to smoke along the way gave us our word "stogy." Seriously. We have the American critic H.L. Mencken to thank for reporting these facts.

Menken, known in his day as "the Sage of Baltimore," is remembered for his many-volume treatise *The American Language*, and for his laughter-filled reporting on the famous "Scopes Trial" in 1925, a legal case in which a public high school science teacher, John Scopes, was accused of violating the law by teaching his students about Darwin's Theory of Evolution.

"Dashboard dining."

MARGARET SHERIDAN (1946–)

*A*RECENT SURVEY ASKED DRIVERS TO NAME WHAT THEY believe most distracts them when they are behind the wheel on the road. The winner was not phoning or texting, but rather eating—picnicking and operating a motor vehicle simultaneously. Eighty-three percent of those surveyed admitted that they drink coffee, juice, or soft drinks and seventy percent admitted that they eat while driving. No one aware of the rapid growth of those drive-through lanes at fast-food restaurants will be surprised by any of this. Some drivers even responded that they are eager for the day when cars become equipped with microwave ovens.

The list of deadly car cookery includes tacos, condiment-heavy burgers, anything barbequed, greasy fried chicken, jelly donuts, and melty chocolate. But it isn't the eating that kills people, it's the spills. We instinctively react to a spill by lurching and flailing about to protect our clothes (or ourselves from hot-drink burns).

We have restaurant columnist Margaret Sheridan to thank for the amusing (and accurate) "dashboard dining." She coined the phrase for "Banquets on a Budget," a December, 1985, column written for the *Chicago Tribune*: "Heaven is a bag of Ben's addictive french-fried shrimp. They're juicy, hot and non-greasy and make dashboard dining a delight."

"*Flew off the handle.*"

THOMAS CHANDLER HALIBURTON (1796–1865)

T HIS SAYING TAKES US BACK TO PIONEER DAYS WHEN AN axe was not something purchased from the local hardware store. The head or business end of the ax was purchased, but the wooden handles were whittled by each woodsman and fitted to the head. Sometimes, perhaps often, a poorly fitted head would slip off the handle while the ax was being wheeled through the air. That could be dangerous for anyone standing nearby, to say the least. And because the ax head was out of control, the analogy with losing one's temper comes readily to mind.

The Canadian lawyer, judge, and businessman Thomas Haliburton is remembered today as the author of a highly popular series of humorous sketches that appeared in *The Nova Scotian* and that were later collected in several published volumes. The first appearance of our phrase appears in Halliburton's 1843 collection, *The Attaché or Sam Slick in England*: "You never see such a crotchety old critter in your life as he is. He flies right off the handle for nothing."

"Shazam!"

WILLIAM H. PARKER, JR. (DIED 1963)

"SHAZAM," YOU SAY, IS NOT A PHRASE—IT'S A SINGLE WORD. Actually, though it is an acronym, "S-h-a-z-a-m," and stands for the following biblical and mythological ancients: Solomon, Hercules, Atlas, Zeus, Achilles, and Mercury. Today we use the word as an interjection to announce a sudden change (much like a magician's "presto!"). We have forgotten the comic-book origin of Shazam, a comic-book character in the 1940's and the invention of comic-book writer Bill Parker.

The backstory was this: an orphaned newsboy named Billy Batson found an ancient wizard in a forgotten nook of an abandoned subway station. The wizard announced that as his days of fighting injustice were at an end, Billy was to be his successor. Whenever the boy would pronounce the wizard's name, Shazam, he would be transformed into the world's mightiest mortal, Captain Marvel.

The Captain's adventures were chronicled in *Whiz Comics*, and during the golden age of the comic book—the 1940's—*Whiz Comics* was incredibly popular. Its sales were enormous by any publishing standard, eclipsing even the previously most popular *Action Comics*, which featured the adventures of Superman, the Man of Steel. As there was little to choose between the two super heroes, a possible reason might be that the young readers (and purchasers) of comic books found the earnest young Billy Batson more appealing than that adult neurotic Clark Kent.

"You fink!"

GEORGE ADE (1866–1944)

T HE EXPERTS CANNOT TELL US WHERE THE WORD "FINK" originated, but we do know that its first appearance in print was in George Ade's 1903 memoir, *People You Know*: "Anyone who goes against the Faculty single-handed is a Fink." Ade was using one of our word's many meanings, "a strike-breaker," but the word has been applied to any unpleasant person for just about any reason, including an informant: "We would have gotten away with it if George hadn't turned fink on us." It is also used as a verb as in "He said he would help, but then he finked out." Yes, and the very worst kind of fink is a "rat fink."

George Ade was an American humorist, a playwright, and a newspaper columnist for the *Chicago Morning News and Record*. His *Tales of the Streets and Town* told the stories of ordinary working people in the bustling metropolis that Chicago had become, and these were collected into a number of best-selling books. He also wrote short stories for *Cosmopolitan Magazine*. Ade's reporting and his fiction celebrated the ordinary American, the "little guy" of the lower middle class, and a number of his books are still in print.

"Free lance."

SIR WALTER SCOTT (1771–1832)

THE FIRST FREE LANCERS WERE MEDIEVAL KNIGHTS WHO sold their fighting skills to wealthy men—men who wanted something done and quite often something villainous. These knights gave "free lancing" its original unsavory reputation.

It was novelist Walter Scott who coined the phrase for these knights in his most popular novel, *Ivanhoe* (1820):

> I offered Richard the service of my Free Lances, and he refused them—I will lead them to Hull, seize on shipping, and embark for Flanders; thanks to the bustling times, a man of action will always find employment. And thou, Waldemar, wilt thou take lance and shield, and lay down thy policies, and wend along with me, and share the fate which God sends us?

Today a freelancer is someone who is self-employed, most often a writer. The term "independent contractor" means the same thing, but lacks the romantic history and image of our "freelancer."

"Charlie horse."

CHARLES GARDNER RADBOURN (1854–1897)

CHARLEY "OLD HOSS" RADBOURN WAS A PROFESSIONAL MAJOR league baseball player—a pitcher—who played for twelve seasons from 1880 to 1891. Although he is seldom referenced today, he won the Triple Crown in 1884 (leading the league in most strikeouts, most wins, and lowest earned-run average). He still holds the record for the most wins in a season, an incredible total of fifty-nine. He was pitching in an unusual number of games that year because the team's other main starter, Charlie Sweeney, was banished from the team in mid-season, and that gave Radbourn double duty with an incredible six-hundred seventy-nine innings pitched.

In his twelve seasons, Radbourn pitched for the Buffalo Bisons, the Providence Grays, the Boston Bean-Eaters, the Boston Reds, and the Cincinnati Reds. He was inducted into the Baseball Hall of Fame in 1939.

According to lexicographer Michael Quinion, Radbourn suffered from recurring and highly painful leg cramps. Thus, Charlie "Old Hoss" Radbourn is the source of "Charlie horse," our current name for that condition.

"Necessity is the mother of invention."

RICHARD FRANCK (1624–1708)

ICHARD FRANK IS ANOTHER OF OUR ORIGINAL PHRASE makers who was a military man as well as an author. He was a captain in the British army and the author of *Northern Memoirs* (written in 1658 but not published until 1694). It was a book of highly elaborate reflections on his travels in Scotland with special emphasis on his experiences there as an avid fisherman. Interestingly, a second edition published in 1821 included an introduction by novelist Sir Walter Scott.

This book gives us the first published record of two well-known sayings: "Necessity is the mother of invention" and "Art imitates nature."

When the subject is invention or inventors, we immediately think of America's greatest practitioner, Thomas Edison, who is remembered for his "Genius is one percent inspiration, ninety-nine percent perspiration." He was also quoted for this: "To invent, you need a good imagination and a pile of junk."

And last, just for the fun of it, this quote from the American humorist and author Jarod Kintz: "I think the two greatest inventions in the history of mankind are the remote control and the fingernail clipper. Now, if someone could just combine those two, I'd be very eager to clip my nails from across the room."

"Nothing to fear but fear itself."

FRANKLIN DELANO ROOSEVELT (1882–1945)

HE THIRTY-SECOND PRESIDENT OF THE UNITED STATES was as often referenced by his initials, FDR, as by his full name. The only American president to serve more than two terms, he led the country through the Great Depression of the 1930s and the World War of the 1940s. During his first one-hundred days in office, he spearheaded a number of reforms and initiatives that became known as the "New Deal." Then, following the Japanese attack on Pearl Harbor in 1941, he brought the USA into the war.

In his first inaugural address, broadcast over the radio, FDR tried to revive the flagging spirits of the citizenry with unvarnished optimism about the future: "The only thing we have to fear is fear itself." The wording was original and has been quoted countless times since. The idea, however, is as old as the Old Testament, for in *Proverbs* 3:25 we read, "Be not afraid of fear."

A number of other writers can be cited as having expressed the thought. Some of these:

"The thing of which I have most fear is fear." Montaigne (1533–1592)

"Nothing is terrible except fear itself." Francis Bacon (1561–1626)

"The only thing I am afraid of is fear." The Duke of Wellington (1814–1852)

"Nothing is so much to be feared as fear." Henry David Thoreau (1817–1862)

The thought was not new, but it is said to have given the president's listeners a much need morale boost.

"No bones about it."

DESIDERIUS ERASMUS ROTERODAMUS (1466–1536)

ETYMOLOGISTS TELL US THAT THIS PHRASE RELATES TO THE act of not making any objection when eating stew (or soup) with bones in it. It now has been generalized to mean there is no doubt in the matter. For example, "Make no bones about it, he cheats at cards." In other words, it is an assertion that is easy to swallow.

Erasmus, a Dutch humanist during the years of the Protestant Reformation, was a Catholic priest and noted theologian. As he worked for compromise, his so-called "Middle Way" angered both Catholic and Protestant theologians. He gave us our first published instance of the use of our phrase in his *Paraphrases of Luke* (published 1548): "Abraham, when commanded to sacrifice his son Isaac, made no bones about it, but went to offer up his son."

Our phrase makers have found many uses for "bones." A doctor is a "saw bones." A thin person is a "bag of bones" or "just skin and bones." The bold have "backbone." Simplification gives us "just the bare bones." The idle man is a "lazy bones." To study is to "bone up on" the subject. A stupid notion is a "bone-headed idea." The pirate flags displayed a skull and "crossbones." And finally, dice are often referred to "bones."

"A fly in the ointment."

KING SOLOMON (10TH CENTURY B.C.)

*W*E DO NOT HEAR MUCH ABOUT OINTMENTS THESE days, so we should specify that these are creamy skin medications, and of course we hardly want to find a fly in our ointment. The phrase came to stand for any small flaw that ruins the whole.

It is a surprisingly ancient saying. In the Old Testament, *Ecclesiastes 10:1*, we find, "Dead flies cause the ointment of the apothecary to send forth a stinking savor: so doth a little folly in him that is in reputation for wisdom and honor."

Ecclesiastes is thought to have been the work of ancient Israel's King Solomon, who ascended the throne upon the death of his father, King David. It is famous for its declaration that human life is futile, fleeting, and in itself, meaningless. "Vanity of vanities; all is vanity."

The first example in print of the usual wording of our phrase is found in the English moralist John Norris's 1707 tract, *A Practical Treatise Concerning Humility*. The relevant passage deserves quoting at some length:

> All our Goodness without Humility is nothing worth, for Pride spoils all our excellences, covers and buries them as Charity does our sins, utterly defaces the Beauty of all our Virtues, and ruins all our good works, not only those which are done in the spirit of Pride, and from a principle of Vanity, but even all the rest so far as concerns any Character or Denomination of Goodness that might accrue to us from them. Tis that Dead Fly in the Ointment of the Apothecary which causes it to send forth an ill favor.

"A horse of another color."

WILLIAM SHAKESPEARE (1564–1616)

W HEN SOMEONE IS SURPRISED BY AN UNEXPECTED turn of meaning, he or she might exclaim, "But that's a horse of a different color!" We might well wonder where such an odd exclamation comes from.

Well. During medieval tournaments, the participating knights-in-armor were identified by the color of the horses they rode (their faces being covered by helmets with visors, that is, armored plates with eye-holes). Disappointed backers of a given knight might lament that the contest had been awarded to a horse of "another" (that is the "wrong") color.

The first published reference to this notion occurs in Act II, Scene 3 of Shakespeare's Christmas play, *Twelfth Night*:

SIR TOBY BELCH: He shall think, by the letters that thou wilt drop, that they come from my niece, and that she's in love with him.

MARIA: My purpose is, indeed, a horse of that color.

Some etymologists have suggested a different source. In Berkshire England, there is an enormous (two-acre) outline of a galloping white horse cut into the turf of a hillside during prehistoric times. Depending upon the season, grass tends to turn the figure from pure white to a greenish hue (making this horse, of course, somewhat of a different color). The local residents periodically clear the horse of the overgrowth.

As a final note on this, the English journalist and poet G.K. Chesterton celebrated the ancient horse-figure in his 1911 epic poem, *The Ballad of the White Horse*.

"Born with a silver spoon in his mouth."

PETER MOTTEUX (1663–1718)

THE EARLIEST SPOONS WERE MADE OF WOOD (THE WORD derives from the Anglo-Saxon *spon*, "chip of wood"), and later spoons were of pewter. Later still, godparents presented a silver spoon to their godchildren during the christening ceremony (at least it was practiced among those who could afford the expense).

The earliest appearance of our saying about silver spoons appears in Motteux's 1701 retelling of Cervantes' classic 1605 novel *Don Quixote* (the phrase does not appear in the original): "Not all is gold that glitters, and every man was not born with a silver spoon in his mouth." The silver spoon, of course, indicates hereditary wealth that does not have to be earned.

Our phrase invites parody. A few examples: The Duke of Bedford (d. 2002) joked that he was born with "a silver-plated spoon" in his mouth. And the English rock band The Who, in the 1966 single, "The Substitute," sings of "being born with a plastic spoon in my mouth." Most famously, Texas State-Treasurer Ann Richards, speaking at the 1988 Democratic National Convention, said of President George H.W. Bush, "Poor George. He can't help it. He was born with a silver foot in his mouth."

"Six of one, half-a-dozen of the other."

FREDERICK MARRYAT (1792–1848)

M ARRYAT WAS BOTH A NOVELIST AND A CAPTAIN IN the English Royal navy. During his service in the navy, he developed a system of flag signaling that is still in use today. And as a novelist, he was one of the first to popularize the stories about life at sea. His experiences on warships supplied him with the material he needed to capture both the romance of service on a warship as well as the dangers.

In his 1836 novel *The Pirate*, Captain Marryat was first to record the phrase about sixes and half-dozens (he may have invented the phrase):

> "Why, how often do you mean to get spliced, Bill? You've a wife in every State, to my sartin knowledge."
>
> "I ain't got one at Liverpool, Jack."
>
> "Any port in a storm. But I say, Bill, did any of your wives ever have twins?"
>
> "I knows the women, but I never knows the children. It's just six of one and half-a-dozen of the other; ain't it?"

Of course the phrase means "no difference" or "nothing to choose between two alternatives."

And one final quote, these angry words of America's former Secretary of State for which she will forever be remembered: "What *difference*, at this point, does it *make*?"

"Smoke-Filled Room."

KIRKE LARUE SIMPSON (1881–1971)

K IRKE SIMPSON, AFTER SERVING AS A SOLDIER IN THE Spanish American War of 1889, achieved distinction for his "The Unknown Soldier," a news report that became a classic. The story celebrated the monument in Washington D.C. dedicated to the memory of all soldiers killed in wars, especially those whose names had been lost to memory.

Known as "the reporter's reporter," Simpson was the first Associated Press reporter to have a bi-line, and the first to win a Pulitzer Prize for the A.P.

When the 1920 Republican convention at the Chicago Coliseum became deadlocked, a group of United States senators met secretly at the Blackstone Hotel to work out a deal. After countless votes, the convention finally settled on Warren G. Harding as the nominee, a little-known candidate who had been selected in that "smoke-filled room." The phrase "smoke-filled room" was coined by Simpson while reporting to the public on those cigar-smoking power brokers at the Blackstone hotel.

Final note: Because "Unknown *Soldier*" was thought to be too exclusive (excluding "sailors," for example), this monument is now called "The Tomb of the Unknowns."

"Sour grapes."

AESOP (620–560 BC)

ESOP, AS MOST OF US LEARNED AT SOME POINT, WAS ancient Greece's great collector of fables. He was a former slave from the region of Thrace (now known as the Balkan Peninsula). Aesop's stories were passed along by word of mouth until the invention of writing made such collections more permanent. Aesop's *Fables* was transcribed in about 300 BC by the Greek philosopher Demetrius Phalereus (350–280 BC).

The story known as "The Fox and Grapes" tells of a fox who sees delicious-looking grapes hanging from an overhead vine. Hoping to assuage his hunger and quench his thirst, he leaps for them several times, but falls short each time by just a few inches. Finally the fox gives up. As he walks away, he is heard to remark that "No doubt, those grapes were sour anyway." And Aesop's moral? "It is easy to despise what you cannot get."

We now use "sour grapes" to contradict an envious and belittling remark. It should be noted, however, that Jean de La Fontaine, the French poet and also an author of fables, thought the fox was admirable because he chose indifference over complaining.

"Seeing is believing.

JOHN CLARK (1596–1658)

OST READERS WHO ARE FAMILIAR WITH THE BIBLICAL *New Testament* will trace this proverb to chapter 20 of the *Gospel of John*. There we read that after the Resurrection, when Jesus first appeared to his inner circle, the apostle Thomas was not present. He did not believe what the others reported to him, and this has given us our catchphrase "doubting Thomas," referring to the skeptic who will not believe a report that is not part of his personal experience. This is not the source of "Seeing is believing," however. As Jesus said to Thomas, "Blessed are they that have not seen and yet have believed." That is an entirely different thought.

John Clark was an English schoolmaster who in 1639 published a book of proverbs for schoolchildren: *Proverbs English and Latin*. A few examples: "The pot calling the kettle black." "To forget a wrong is the best revenge." "Early to bed, early to rise, makes a man healthy, wealthy, and wise." (Yes, Benjamin Franklin lifted the saying from Clark's book). Clark's *Proverbs* gives us the first published instance in English of "Seeing is believing," a maxim he borrowed from the French essayist Montaigne (1533–1592).

"*Dibs on.*"

LEON MARCUS URIS (1924–2003)

"DIBS"? THE WORD IS FROM A ONCE POPULAR (BUT NOW forgotten) children's game, "dibstones," the object of which was to toss a stone at your opponent's stone—somewhat akin to the game of "lagging" or tossing marbles. Hitting the opponent's stone gave a player possession of that stone, and so, to have "dibs on" means to have first claim on something that is available (or "up for grabs" as another catchphrase expresses it).

L.M. Uris was an American novelist who served in the Marine Corps during World War II. His stories center on recent history and reflect his military experiences. His best known work was *Exodus* (1958), which related the story of the founding of the State of Israel. It was made into an award-winning 1960 movie starring Paul Newman. The theme music was later made into a hit single with lyrics written by singer Pat Boone.

Battle Cry (1953) gave us our first published reference to our phrase: "Two bottles of beer were issued to all enlisted men. 'Dibs on your beer, Mary.'"

"An arm and a leg."

BEULAH KARNEY MULLEN (1899–1991)

HERE IS A STORY ABOUT THE ORIGIN OF THIS PHRASE THAT is worth retelling. It has to do with the way portrait painters once calculated the price they would charge for a portrait. "Head and shoulders only" was the least expensive option, including arms raised the price, and the choice of "legs and all" was the most costly. There is no evidence that there is any truth in this, except the obvious fact that artists charged more for larger pictures.

The first published appearance of our phrase is to be found in the column of *Long Beach Independent* food-editor Beulah Karney in December of 1949. As she listed her Christmas recipe suggestions for homemakers, she remarked that none of the ideas would "cost an arm and a leg."

We note in passing that the French have a similar saying in "Ça coûte les yeux de la tête" ("It costs the eyes from one's head.") More seriously, some etymologists have suggested that the phrase ultimately derives from the high cost to servicemen injured in fighting our wars.

"*Age before beauty.*"

CLARE BOOTHE LUCE (1903–1987)

*I*N YEARS PAST, WHEN RULES OF COURTESY WERE MORE routinely followed, it was customary for younger people to defer to their elders. An example of this was allowing the older person to enter a doorway first. The older persons would often remark "age before beauty" to show their approval that good manners had been shown.

The experts have not been able to trace the true origin of this phrase, but including it here gives us the excuse to relate the following anecdote. According to author Robert Benchley (who claimed to have been standing nearby and to have heard what was said), author and diplomat Clare Booth Luce and the poet and satirist Dorothy Parker were about to enter a hotel dining room together. Luce stopped and offered to allow her companion to enter first. She used our catchphrase, "Age before beauty." Parker did not miss a beat: "And pearls before swine," she said. (The reference was to Jesus' admonition, "Do not give what is holy to the dogs; nor cast your pearls before swine" (*Matthew* 7:6).

Some other notable responses to "Age before beauty" are "Dust before the broom," "Monkeys before people," and (referring to Anna Sewell's 1877 novel *Black Beauty*) "*Beauty*, the horse?"

"Dead cat bounce."

WONG SULONG (1947–)

*I*S IT TRUE THAT EVEN A DEAD CAT WILL BOUNCE IF IT FALLS far enough? Whether true or not, the idea is that recoveries can be misleading, temporary, and a trap for the unwary. The phrase is mainly used by speculators and brokers in stocks and commodities where there are continuous variations in price as demand ebbs and flows. When the price of one of these items has a long and uninterrupted fall, it is not unusual for there to be, at some point, a halt to the slide and a temporary recovery. Anyone who believes this is a sign of a continuing price revival, and who buys in, then falls victim to the "dead cat bounce."

Wong Sulong, a native of Malaysia, studied economics at the University of London, graduating in 1972. He then took a position as a business correspondent for the Australian Broadcasting Corporation and the *Financial Times*. During the recession of 1985, when the markets in Singapore and Malaysia took a beating and prices fell drastically, there was a point at which prices bounced back. According to Sulong, this was a prime example of the "dead cat bounce." The expression caught on and, whether referring to one's health, love life, or career, it has been used on innumerable occasions when a brief recovery is merely temporary, and the long-term decline then resumes.

"The blind side."

HAL HIGDON (1931–)

I N MAJOR SPORTS, ESPECIALLY AMERICAN FOOTBALL, TO BE blindsided is to be looking one way and to be hit (tackled, blocked, or otherwise struck) by another player coming from the other direction, the direction we were not attending to. Most of us have been blindsided—if not in sports, then in life. That is, we have been totally surprised, shocked, and often horribly embarrassed or outraged by some unforeseen news. An example? "His fiancée was seeing other men, and when he learned about it he felt totally blindsided."

Hal Higdon, an American journalist, author, and champion runner, was the first to introduce our phrase to the reading public. In a 1968 article for *Pro Football USA*, we find: "Usually it is the quarterback who gets blind-sided as he is about to pass."

Many readers will immediately remember the 2009 award-winning film, *The Blind Side,* starring actress Sandra Bullock. Based on the 2006 Michael Lewis book, *The Blindside: Evolution of a Game,* the movie tells the story of Michael Oher, an offensive lineman who now plays for the Baltimore Ravens. As a high-school player loaded with talent, Oher had difficulty adjusting to the violence that football required of him. Finally, the concept of protecting the quarterback's blindside brought him into the game. The film was nominated for the Best Picture Academy Award.

And while we are at it, who's got your back?

"Pot head."

NORMAN KINGSLEY MAILER (1923–2007)

SOMEHOW THE WORD "HEAD," AMONG ITS COUNTLESS meanings, came to denote a user or enthusiast. Thus the youngster who equips his stereo with massive bass speakers is referred to as a "base head," and a cocaine addict is a "crack head." The American author Norman Mailer gave us the first published reference to "head" with this meaning. In his 1961 essay collection, *Advertisements for Myself,* we find: "There was a horde: movie stars who left early, councilors, pot heads (discreet to be sure), hoodlums, and so on."

"Head" is one of the dictionary's most versatile words. Just the example of "stupidity" will give us the flavor of this. We have "chuckle headed," "knuckle heads," "air heads," "chowder head," "bone headed," "dunder heads," "fat head," "lunk head," and "pin heads." And that is our "heads up" for this subject.

"*Fat cat.*"

FRANK RICHARDSON KENT (1877–1958)

I N POLITICS, A "FAT CAT" IS A WEALTHY DONOR. HIS beneficiaries call him an "angel" (borrowing the word from the term used for financial backer of a theatrical production), but to others he is simply a "big money man." What the fat cats buy with these donations is the problem. In the American campaign finance system, money buys the fat cat access, influence, and power over appointments. This leads to corruption and the abuse of public power.

Politics aside, we also use "fat cat" to describe the rich, greedy, and lazy person who is able to relax and live off the labor of others.

The American journalist and columnist Frank Kent who—though a Democrat himself—was deeply critical of the so-called "New Deal" policies of President Franklin Delano Roosevelt. In an essay that appeared in the *American Mercury* magazine Kent wrote:

> A Fat Cat is a man of large means and no political experience who having reached middle age, and success in business, and finding no further thrill of satisfaction in the mere piling up of more millions, develops a yearning for some sort of public honor and is willing to pay for it. The machine has what it seeks, public honor, and he has the money the machine needs

That definition gave us our first look at the phrase, "fat cat."

"A slap on the back."

RICHARD STEELE (1672–1729)

*I*T IS INTERESTING TO NOTE THAT IN OUR LANGUAGE, A "SLAP" can be good or bad depending on the context. We all would like to have the boss give us a slap on the back. But we do not want "a slap in the face" or to be "slapped down." Too many such slaps might make us "slap happy." It would be much better to have a token "slap on the wrist."

Sir Richard Steele was an Irish politician and Member of Parliament, but he is most remembered for *The Spectator*, the periodical he founded in 1711 along with Joseph Addison (1672–1719). However, it was in an earlier of Steele's journals, *The Tattler*, that we find the earliest published reference to our phrase. In an essay published in 1709 we find: "One got behind me in the interim, and hit me a sound slap on the back." Obviously, the slap on the back had not yet acquired its happier meaning.

"*Yada yada yada.*"

LEONARD ALFRED SCHNEIDER (1925–1966)

TODAY STAND-UP COMEDIAN SCHNEIDER, BETTER KNOWN by his stage name Lenny Bruce, is remembered for his use of religion, politics, and sex as subject material for his jokes— interlaced with tons of obscenities. In this he was a pioneer of sorts. In truth, I caught Bruce's act in a Chicago nightclub many years ago. The next day the Chicago police arrested Bruce for doing some of the things he had joked about the night before.

Bruce introduced us to the catchphrase "Yada yada yada," which means the same as "blah blah blah," "and so on and so forth," "etcetera, etcetera, etcetera," or columnist Wesley Pruden's "jaw jaw." These signal to one's listeners that the speaker is skipping a part of the story that won't be told, usually because it is irrelevant to the purpose at hand. Three more terms for meaningless chatter that must be included here are "argle-bargle," "foofaraw," and "kerfuffle," each of which mean a pointless argument about a trivial matter.

We note also that "Yada Yada" was the title of a 1997 episode of the American television situation-comedy series, *Seinfeld*, starring stand-up comedian Jerry Seinfeld. The program with our phrase as its title won an Emmy for its writers Peter Mehlman and Jill Franklyn.

"Like a fox guarding the henhouse."

DECIMUS IUNIUS IUVENALIS. (55–127 AD)

THE THOUGHT EXPRESSED IN THIS PHRASE IS A VERY ancient one and has taken many forms. One example: "The wolf guarding the sheep." Today, the basic idea is repeated in worries about "self-regulation," "conflicts of interest," and when industry "insiders" are put in charge of policing that industry. It happens. As columnist John Fund has recently asked, "Who's watching the watchers?"

Juvenal, the foremost satirical poet of ancient Rome, was (as far as can be determined) the first to express this idea with his "*Quis custodiet ipsos custodes*?" ("Who will guard the guards?" from *Satire VI*, 347). There, surprisingly enough, Juvenal is discussing marital infidelity rather than political or commercial corruption.

This brings us to the modern day con-man (the "sharper" of yesterday), who hopes to be put in charge of his victim's bank account like the fox who hopes to be put in control of the victim's chicken coop.

"*Go figure.*"

FREDA BRIGHT (1929–)

N O KIDDING!" OR "ARE YOU KIDDING ME?" "WELL, I'LL BE damned" (or softened to "I'll be darned," or just "Well, I'll be…"), "You don't say." "Who knew?" "Surprise, surprise!" and "Go figure!" In other words, "Let's try to explain that." "Go figure" was originally introduced to readers in novelist Bright's 1988 novel, *Singular Women*, the story of a husband-hunting contest: "Hank Sayer would develop into a dashing journalist. Go figure!" Then we have the 2005 made-for-television Walt Disney movie, *Go Figure*.

And here's an amusing passage well worth quoting at some length because it gives us the flavor of author Freda Bright's work:

In the late 1600s the finest instruments originated from three rural families whose workshops were side by side in the Italian village of Cremona. First were the Amatis, and outside their shop hung a sign: "The Best Violins in All Italy." Not to be outdone, their next-door neighbors, the family Guarnerius, hung a bolder sign proclaiming: "The Best Violins in All the World!" At the end of the street was the workshop of Anton Stradivarius, and on its front door was a simple notice which read: "The best violins on the block."

"By the skin of my teeth."

MOSES (1520–1400 BC)

WE STILL HEAR, FROM TIME TO TIME, OF SOMEONE WHO claims to have escaped by "the skin of my teeth." Well, teeth, having no skin, this gives us the meaning of an extremely close call: "It missed us by a hair," a "close shave," a "narrow escape," and so on.

Our phrase is surprisingly old, one of our oldest, in fact. Its earliest recorded appearance is found in the Hebrew Bible's *Book of Job*," which has been ascribed to Moses, the most important of Judaism's prophets. Job, you will recall, lost his family, his possessions, and his health at the hands of Satan. In Chapter 19 we find:

> All my intimate friends detest me; those I love have turned against me. I am nothing but skin and bones; I have escaped only by the skin of my teeth.
>
> Have pity on me, my friends, have pity, for the hand of God has struck me.

For those unfamiliar with the story, in the end Job's health, wealth, and family are restored to him.

One sidelight of this is the 1941 Pulitzer-Prize winning drama *The Skin of Our Teeth* by Author Thornton Wilder. The play tells the story of the suburban couple George and Maggie Antrobus, married for five thousand years, and who, while saving the world from catastrophe and inventing things like the alphabet, have managed to survive—yes—by the skin of their teeth.

"Keep on Truckin'."

ROBERT DENNIS CRUMB (1943–)

THE COMMAND TO "KEEP ON TRUCKIN'" ORIGINATED IN A poster by Hall-of-Fame cartoonist Crumb in 1968. It was published in the underground comic book, *Zap Comix*. The cartoon shows a ground-level view of a group of smiling men happily marching forward in a line. Crumb later said the cartoon was "the curse of my life."

Why? Crumb considered himself a loyal member of the 1960's counter culture. The surprising popularity of this single cartoon threatened to make him seem "mainstream" and a part of the popular culture of the squares. He saw it on tee-shirts, posters, and other such merchandise (for which, by the way, he received no royalties). He could not live with what he saw as an attack on his reputation. He said he did not want to become "America's best loved hippy artist." And so he turned the subject of his art to the perverse sexual images with which he is now most often associated.

After the hippy era, Crumb turned to biographical subjects. This work was published in *Weirdo* (1981–1993), a magazine he founded, and which has been cited as one of the best publications of the alternative comics era.

"*Person of interest.*"

JOHN ASHCROFT (1942–)

*W*HEN DID WE START SAYING "PERSON OF INTEREST" instead of "suspect" and why did we change? "Suspect" has a clear definition (as do "target," "accomplice," "witness" and "subject") but "person of interest" has no official or legal meaning. Why the change?

Ashcroft, as Attorney General of the United States, popularized the use of this phrase while investigating the anthrax attacks of 2001. Letters laced with this poison were sent to offices of two Senators and to several media offices. Five people died and a number of others were infected but recovered. In a press conference, Ashcroft noted that Steven Hatfill (an expert on viruses) was a "person of interest" in the case. However, no charges were ever brought against Hatfill, and he eventually sued Ashcroft and the Justice Department for violating his rights. The Justice Department settled the case for 5.8 million dollars.

Meanwhile, "person of interest" caught on with crime reporters, and most law enforcement agencies then adopted the term. It permits the publication of a name associated with a crime without requiring the police to define exactly what interests them about that person. Who could resist a form of hedging that does not seem like hedging?

"*Victory garden.*"

SAMUEL WINFIELD LEWIS (1930–)

O LDER READERS WILL REMEMBER WORLD WAR II VICTORY gardens and may well have planted such a garden or at least helped with one. The gardens were part of what was called "the war effort" on the "home front." That war was a "total war," and everyday life for those at home was radically changed. Barrels graced every corner for the collection of scrap-metal, children in our schools joined the "Write a Fighter Corps" and penned letters to relatives overseas as a school assignment. Food, gasoline, and clothing were rationed. Women were enlisted in the war effort as never before. Women Air-Service Pilots (Wasps) delivered fighter aircraft from the factories to military bases. Women took over for the men in factories, as one song of the day, "Rosie the Riveter," celebrated:

> Rosie's got a boy friend Charlie
> Charlie he's a Marine
> Rosie is protecting Charlie
> Working overtime on her riveting machine

The "victory gardens" were vegetable gardens planted at private residences and public parks to reduce the pressure on the food supply. In 1943, for example, it was reported that twenty-million such gardens had produced eight million tons of food.

Samuel Lewis is the American diplomat (now retired) who gave us an early mention of these gardens in a 1942 letter: "Why doesn't she lie low and work in her victory-garden?"

"*Same old same old.*"

MALCOLM JOHN "MAC" REBENNACK, JR. (1940–)

*U*SUALLY FOR A SONG LYRIC, THE COMPOSER WILL PICK up a phrase popular on the street and borrow it for the song. There are plenty of examples. "One-Horse Town" gave songwriter Bernie Taupin the title for a 1976 Elton John hit. The Fifth Dimension made the charts with their single "Up, Up and Away." "Love Makes the World Go 'Round" was the theme song for the 1961 Hollywood musical, *Carnival*. The 1985 musical version of Victor Hugo's *Les Miserable* included a song with the title "At the End of the Day." Song-writer Michael Franks used "Monkey See—Monkey Do" in the title and lyric of his 1976 hit song. Well, this list could be extended to any length desired.

The point here is that, for once anyway, the song introduced to the public a phrase that only afterward became popular in everyday usage. When we are asked about an annoying situation that never seems to change, we often reply, "Oh, well—same old same old." Here are, in part, the words to Rebennack's hit tune:

> 'Cause do I love you,
> Oh, I do,
> And I'm going to 'til I'm gone.
> But if you think that I can stay in this
> same old, same old,
> Well, I don't.

"Straw man."

STUART CHASE (1888–1985)

"STRAW MAN" HAS A NUMBER OF MEANINGS, BUT HERE THE focus is on the fallacy of informal logic with that name. It is a trick in argumentation to misrepresent one's opponent's position and to assert something similar but weaker and easily refuted. These weaker arguments are knocked down as easily as a straw man or scarecrow is knocked over in a field of corn. Also, and incidentally, in England the fallacy is often referred to as an "Aunt Sally."

Stuart Chase was an American engineer and economist whose wide ranging interests and writings included his 1956 *Guides to Straight Thinking*. There we find the first published reference to and explanation of the "straw man" fallacy. The experts in etymology also inform us that Chase was the first to characterize the Roosevelt administration's package of economic reforms and stimulants as "the New Deal" in a 1932 article for *The New Republic*.

Movie fans will point to "Hunk the Scarecrow" in the classic 1939 film *The Wizard of Oz* as their favorite straw man. And, of course, Batman fans will point to "the Scarecrow," a super-villain in Batman comics and films.

Last, there is this reference from British poet T.S. Eliot's 1922 classic poem, "The Hollow Men":

> We are the hollow men
> We are the stuffed men
> Leaning together
> Headpiece filled with straw. Alas!

"Word for word."

GEOFFREY CHAUCER (1343–1400)

ONCE AGAIN WE RETURN TO CHAUCER FOR ONE OUR EARLY references. This time it is his "The Legend of Dido" from *The Legend of Good Women* (1385), a lengthy poem that relates stories of admirable women in history and myth in the form of poetic dream visions. According to legend, Dido was the founder and first Queen of Carthage (modern-day Tunisia). The Roman poet Virgil gives an account of her reign in his epic poem, *The Aeneid* (29–19 BC).

We say something is "word for word" when referring to an exact quotation. It is a "verbatim" quote, to use a more formal word for this. Also, we note in passing. "Word for Word" is the name of a children's board game.

The quotation from "The Legend of Dido": "I could follow word for word Virgil, but it would last all too long while." (That presents Chaucer's words in modern English, but the quote is still word for word.)

Other ways of expressing the thought behind this phrase include "verbatim report," "faithful to the original," "in identical words," and "exact transcript." Also, we note in passing, "Word for Word" is the name of a children's board game.

"*Stock market bubble.*"

CHARLES MACKAY (1812–1889)

SOME READERS MAY HAVE BEEN HURT FINANCIALLY IN THE late nineteen-nineties when the stock market, powered by the rapid growth of the new internet companies, became wildly oversold. Speculators had poured money into these new-fangled businesses until the market reacted. The subsequent crash has become known as the "dot.com bubble." And why "bubble"? That is simply because bubbles burst.

Charles Mackey was a Scottish journalist, novelist, poet, and song writer who is remembered today for his ground-breaking study of the infamous "tulip mania" that engulfed Holland in in the sixteen-thirties. Tulips were something new in the world of flowering plants—color-ful flowers that could tolerate the harsher weather of northern lands. Tulips took Holland by storm, and became something of a status symbol for gardeners. Prices for the bulbs were driven up to ridiculous heights. When the bubble burst, the entire Dutch economy collapsed.

This sad story, and his general theory of theory of speculative bubbles, was popularized in 1841 in Mackey's book *Extraordinary Popular Delusions and the Madness of Crowds*. And, of course, the greatest stock-market bubble of the twentieth century burst in 1929, leading the world into the great depression of the nineteen thirties.

"Rent seeking."

GORDON TULLOCK (1922–)

WHEN I FIRST SAW THIS PHRASE, IT STRUCK ME AS simple enough, but I did not have a clue as to what it might mean. A bit of investigating quickly gave me the answer: "rent seeking" is the attempt to get money without working for it. It is getting "something for nothing"— "free money" or "free lunch." For example, if a farmer writes a letter to his congressman asking for his support for a farm subsidy bill that will mean more money in the farmer's pocket (without further effort on the farmer's part) then the farmer is "rent seeking." Similarly, if a racketeer sells "protection" to a shopkeeper (meaning protection from the mobster's own gang), then he is "rent seeking." Our government lobbyists are professional rent seekers. Business practices aimed at securing monopoly control over a given market, or tariff protection, or the imposition of quotas are also examples.

Gordon Tullock, now retired, was a Professor of Law and Economics at George Mason University. He is famous for applying economic theory to politics. The concept of "rent seeking" is his best known contribution in that area. In his theory, restrictions on free enterprise such as licensing, minimum wage laws, copyrights, certi-fication, patent protection, housing projects for the poor, patronage (favors for political support), and government redistribution by way of entitlement spending (food stamps, for example) are all "rent seek-ing" arrangements for the recipients.

"Dead ringer."

JOHN BUCHAN (1875–1940)

OUR WORD "RINGER" HAS THREE COMMON MEANINGS. FIRST we have the person who rings bells. Then there is the secret and dishonest substitute for a less talented competitor. And third, a person who bears a striking resemblance to another. Why "dead"? Well, "dead" also means "exact" as in "it hit dead center" and "she was a dead shot." And so, our phrase means a person who bears a remarkable resemblance to another.

Scotsman John Buchan is most remembered for his novels, especially *The 39 Steps* (1915), which was made into a memorable movie by Alfred Hitchcock in 1935. However, his principle occupation was as a diplomat, propagandist (for the British World War I war effort), and as Prime Minister of Canada. It is in his 1916 novel *Greenmantle* that we find the first published instance of our phrase: "Now you're in these pretty clothes, you're the dead ringer for the brightest kind of American engineer."

It may be unforgivable to repeat the two worst jokes in the history of humor, but here they are (greatly and mercifully abbreviated, for the originals go on interminably). "After the death of the of the cathedral's armless bell ringer (who moved the bells by pushing them with his forehead), the bishop was asked his name. "I don't recall his name," the bishop replied, "but his face rings a bell." The successor bell-ringer was the man's brother, who then also died. This time the bishop replied, "I never knew his name, but he's a dead ringer for his brother."

"Hat tip."

JAMES CECIL HATLOW (1897–1963),

WE HAVE ALL SEEN "HAT TIP" (SOMETIME ABBREVIATED to "HT" or "h/t") on blogs, and sometimes even in mainstream journalism on the internet, to indicate that the person referred to made a contribution to the article, or perhaps even suggested the subject. We may have used "h/t" ourselves. However, tipping one's hat once had an entirely different meaning. In the nineteenth century, a man tipped his hat (raised it slightly) while walking past an acquaintance. We are told that the military salute was derived from this practice.

Jimmy Hatlo was a syndicated cartoonist who in 1929 started a humorous comic strip he named "They'll Do It Every Time." This was a single-paneled (or often double-paneled) cartoon that illustrated the minor mishaps and frustrations of everyday life in the United States. Hatlo quickly ran short of ideas for the feature, and he began asking his readers to send him examples from their own experiences. The cartoonist acknowledged these contributions with a small concluding box that read, "Thanx and a tip of the Hatlo hat to John Doe."

Hatlo's comic strip was immensely popular, and in 1936 went into national syndication with King Features.

"Spaghetti western."

SERGIO LEONE (1929–1989)

*L*EONE DID NOT COIN THE PHRASE "SPAGHETTI WESTERN" for that distinction belongs to the Italian journalist, Alfonso Sancha. However, it was Leone's films in the nineteen-sixties that defined the category. American film-goers will especially remember *A Fistful of Dollars* (1964), *For a Few Dollars More* (1965), and *The Good, the Bad, and the Ugly* (1966), films that launched the career of actor Clint Eastwood. These were followed by the interminably lengthy *Once Upon a Time in the West* (1968) with Jason Robards, Charles Bronson, and the lovable Henry Fonda cast as the heartless villain.

Leone's films were tales of the "American west" that were produced and filmed in Italy. The casts were of various nationalities, and the dialogue was "post synched," that is dubbed over in the native language of each audience the world over. Composer Ennio Morricone's musical score for *Once Upon a Time* has been acclaimed as the finest theme music ever produced for a motion-picture film.

What was it about these movies? Critics point to the complicated plot twists and turns, the unexpected actions of the hero, and the heightened brutality against innocent people—all foreign to the Hollywood Western. In short, it was definitely not John Wayne material.

"*Got my goat.*"

JACK LONDON (1876–1916)

HE PHRASE ABOUT GETTING A GOAT HAS AN UNUSUAL origin. If historians are to be believed, in the nineteenth century goats were often kept in the stables of the high-strung race horses. The goats were said to have a calming effect on the thoroughbreds, and removing these companions would upset the horses and hurt their subsequent performance on the track. It has also been reported that unscrupulous gamblers would remove a goat on the sly, and in that way upset the horse sufficiently to cause it to lose its next race.

Thus "to get one's goat" was generalized to mean "to get one annoyed and angry."

Jack London was American author, journalist, and social activist. "London" was actually the penname of John Griffith Chaney, one of the first of modern writers to make a fortune and achieve international fame by nothing other than publishing fiction. His best known works are his novels *The Call of the Wild* (1903) set during the Klondike gold rush and *The Sea World* (1904) set in San Francisco. In his 1912 novel *Smoke Bellew,* London gave his readers the first published appearance of our phrase "got his goat."

"Cut off your nose to spite your face."

GÉDÉON TALLEMANT (1619–1692)

OW HERE IS AN EXCEEDINGLY VIVID AND GRIM SORT OF saying. What can we make of it? We are told it refers to anger so unreasoned that the attacker ends up hurting himself more than his victim. An example of such self-destructive behavior might be a husband so provoked by his wife's "running around" without him at night that in an uncontrollable fit of anger he wrecks the family car to stop her escapades. However, the husband is a travelling salesman and he needs that car to earn a living.

This is a surprisingly old motto. It traces back to Tallemant's *Historiettes* (short biographies, focused on scandals among aristocrats). There we find this: "Henry IV well knew that to destroy Paris would be to cut off his own nose in taking spite on his face," referring to the Henry who reigned as King of France from 1589 to 1610, a time of massive religious turmoil and upheaval.

Some experts trace our saying to the centuries-earlier Viking raids on Scotland. Nuns in convents, this story says, purposely disfigured their faces by cutting off their noses in order to disgust the raiders and thus preserve their chastity. While this is an interesting story, it does not seem to fit the meaning of "to spite your face." "…to spite the Vikings," would be the more appropriate wording there.

"Holy Grail."

CHRÉTIEN DE TROYES (LATE 12TH CENTURY)

*A*S REPORTED IN THE NEWS RECENTLY AND ACCORDING to infectious disease researcher Katie Ballering of the University of Minnesota, "the Holy Grail of influenza research is a universal flu vaccine." We often see such references to the "Holy Grail" as the highly prized object of a lengthy search or the goal of a prolonged undertaking. But just what is this "Grail"? We have the word "grail" from a Latin word for "dish," but that does not explain the true significance of our phrase.

We must turn to legends of the British King Arthur and his "knights of the round table." After the crucifixion of Jesus, Joseph of Arimathea took possession of the body and captured the last blood droplets in a cup that he then sent to Britain for safe keeping. Centuries later, after the Grail had been lost, King Arthur and his knights were commissioned to search for it.

Chrétien de Troyes was a late twelfth-century French poet and troubadour (composer and performer of lyric poetry) known for his work on Arthurian subjects. We owe most of the story of Arthur and the Round Table to his poetic romances, and he is also our earliest source for Merlin the court magician, Arthur's spouse Guinevere, Sir Lancelot his foremost knight, and the quest to find the Holy Grail.

"Horse sense."

JAMES KIRKE PAULDING (1778–1860)

OUR PHRASE MEANS STRONG, UNUSUALLY ROBUST COMMON sense. Shrewdness. An intuitive grasp of the nature of things. But what has this to do with horses? The idea is that illiterate country people have an innate, practical insight into whatever matter is under discussion—an insight that often puts more learned observers to shame. A parallel phrase for uneducated city dwellers is "street smarts."

J.K. Paulding was a close friend of American author Washington Irving. The two planned several literary projects together, but these eventually came to nothing. Paulding's best-remember work is his 1832 novel, *Westward Ho!* That is where we find the first published appearance of our phrase:

> I'm for Dangerfield, though he hasn't got a pocket handkerchief, and though he can't play on the piano. He's a man of good strong horse sense, and his sister can make a pair of moccasins out of his old boots.

President Martin Van Buren appointed Pauling Secretary of the navy in 1938. After retiring from government service in 1841, he took up farming in New York State and returned to his first love, writing fiction.

"Looking out for number one."

JEREMY BENTHAM (1748–1832)

Consider this simple word "number." Is there another common word in the English language with so many different meanings? The technical definitions in mathematics would fill several pages of this book, and we will ignore those. Even so, the uses of this word in everyday speech defy one's ability to make a complete list.

Examples: we use number in grammar (singular or plural?), for clothing sizes, for identification (social security numbers and so on), for a group ("I'm one of their number"), to identify the issue of a periodical ("It was mentioned in the Christmas number"), a musical composition ("she sang a number from *Oklahoma*), a total (the number of ounces in a quart), a street racket ("numbers game" and "numbers runner"), a repeated argument or excuse ("doing their usual number"), to deceive ("do a number on"), "number cruncher" (one who performs numerous calculations), "numberless" (vast, countless), "take a number" (wait your turn), "your number is up" (you are at death's door), "public enemy number one," "opposite number" (a counterpart), we all hate to phone a "wrong number," and then there is "The Book of Numbers" from the *Hebrew Bible*. Needless to say, this hardly exhausts the list.

Jeremy Bentham was a British expert in the Philosophy of Law. We find the first mention of our featured phrase in a letter he penned in 1791: "It concerns me to take care of number one, and not get into any more scrapes."

And last, from the well-known the New Orleans funeral march: "I want to be in that number, when the Saints go marching in."

"*For the hell of it.*"

PEARL ZANE GREY (1872–1939)

*A*S A PLACE, HELL IS NOT SOMEWHERE WE EVER WANT TO be. However, as a curse word, "hell" is arguably our most popular choice. The complete list would take many pages, but here is a sampling: Go to hell, I'll see you in hell, What the hell, Not a chance in hell, To hell with it, Like hell!, Give 'em hell, It was a hell hole, It was hell on earth, There'll be hell to pay, We were raising hell, All hell broke loose, To hell and back, Hells bells!, Hot (or cold) as hell, Mad as hell, Sorry as all hell, I hope to hell…, Come hell or high water, It played hell with…, and the college fraternities with their "Hell Week." Then there was the 1941 Hollywood movie *Hellzapoppin* based on the Broadway musical of the same name.

Almost any English-speaking author could be picked as our source for a "hell" phrase. Zane Grey's novels and stories of the American West seems as likely a source as any. "For the hell of it" can be found in his 1908 novel *The Last of the Plainsmen.* Over one hundred motion pictures have been filmed based on Gray's fiction, and I would say that is one hell of a record.

"A piece of cake."

FREDERIC OGDEN NASH (1902–1971)

*I*F A TASK WAS EASILY DONE, WE OFTEN SAY IT WAS "A PIECE OF cake" (or sometimes, "easy as pie" or "it was a cakewalk"). Why these dessert items? Well, we eat both for nourishment and for pleasure, but the one course in a full meal that seems devoted almost entirely to enjoyment is our dessert course, which is usually something sweet and delicious.

Ogden Nash was and is America's foremost author of humorous poetry. He is especially remembered for his run-on lines and his oddball rhymes. The earliest published reference to our phrase is found in his 1936 collection of verse, *Primrose Path*: "Her picture's in the papers now and life's a piece of cake."

And what about "cake-walk"? In late nineteenth-century America, "Cake Walks" were held in the South among African Americans. The couple performing the most amusing or skillful strutting steps were awarded the first prize of a cake. The Cake Walks became a staple of the travelling minstrel shows and a familiar entertainment for all Americans. And that gives us our "that takes the cake" to describe something superlatively good (or bad).

"Gave us zilch."

PATRICIA WELLES. (19?–)

"ZIP, ZERO, NADA, NIL, NAUGHT, EMPTY, A CIPHER, NULL, A goose egg, nix." Yes, we have many ways to indicate "nothing," but "zilch"? Well, etymologists tell us this relatively recent addition to our dictionaries was formed from the combination of "zero" and "nil." Some have said the final "ch" comes from "check," but that opinion has not been substantiated by any clear evidence.

For the first printed appearance of our word, we turn to Patricia Welles and her 1967 novel *Babyhip*, a typical sixties story of teenage rebellion. We find "zilch" in this sentence: "Half-starved, no doubt. The old harlot probably fed him zilch." Welles is most remembered for her 1969 novel *Bob and Carol and Ted and Alice*, which was made into an academy award winning film in that same year.

"Boots on the ground."

SIR ROBERT GRAINGER KER THOMPSON (1916–1992)

MILITARY COMMANDERS DREAM OF A WORLD IN WHICH wars might be won without the use of troops fighting on battlefields. Their tactics have included air strikes (bombing and strafing), naval bombardment, long range artillery and missiles, drone attacks, blockades, the use of guerrilla warriors, and sabotage. Experience teaches, however, that military success cannot be achieved without foot troops physically deployed and prepared to engage the enemy in the area of combat.

Journalists of late have been overworking the phrase "boots on the ground" when discussing the complexities of strategies for dealing with serious problems in the Middle Eastern wars and insurrections: the use of chemical or nuclear weapons, fraudulent elections, riots in the streets, and refugees. The United Nations and its member states seem at a loss as to what to do. However, all want to avoid if possible putting "boots on the ground."

Robert Thompson was a British expert on the subject of counter-terrorism. Our experts tell us he is the first to use the phrase "boots on the ground." Later (2003), *Boots on the Ground* was written by journalist Karl Zinsmeister based on his experiences while embedded with the 82nd Airborne Division during the early days of Operation Iraqi Freedom.

"Elephant in the room."

LUDWIG JOSEF JOHANN WITTGENSTEIN (1889–1951)

SOMETIMES, WHEN A GROUP OF PEOPLE ARE DISCUSSING something, there is an unspoken understanding that there is one subject no one will bring into the conversation. It might be something like the embarrassing fact that the husband of the hostess is not present because he was jailed early that morning for driving under the influence. Or, it might be news of divorce proceedings that one of the couples has just recently initiated. That the unmentionable subject is on everyone's mind makes it the "elephant in the room" that no one will acknowledge.

Our expression about the elephant was first used by Cambridge professor Wittgenstein in an abstract philosophical discussion of the impossibility of proving a universal negative.

Unseen elephants have come into play in various ways. Mark Twain's 1882 story "The Stolen White Elephant" gives us the spectacle of detectives trying to find an elephant that was never missing in the first place. In 1935, comedian Jimmy Durante starred in the Broadway musical *Jumbo*. As Durante led a full-grown elephant across the stage, a police officer asked him what he was doing with "that elephant." Durante's deadpan reply, "What elephant?" never failed to bring down the house with laughter.

Finally, for accuracy's sake, Wittgenstein's example was actually a "rhinoceros" in the room.

"Wreak havoc."

DAME AGATHA MARY CLARISSA CHRISTIE (1890–1976)

FIRST, WHAT IS THIS WORD "WREAK"? IT IS ONE OF THE oldest words in our English language and is often confused with the verb "wreck" ("to destroy"). "Wreak" means "to inflict" (punishment or revenge) or "to cause" (damage or disorder). "Havoc" comes to us from the French and means "devastation" or "chaos." And so, to "wreak havoc" is to "inflict ruin." The earliest use of "havoc" was as a military command in the Middle Ages. The word commanded English forces to maximize damage to the enemy by any and all means including pillaging, destroying dwellings, and causing general chaos for the enemy in as many ways as possible.

Agatha Christie was England's best known author of mystery stories during the so-called "golden Age" of crime fiction in the nineteen-twenties. Her detectives—Hercule Poirot, Miss Jane Marple, and Tommy and Tuppence Beresford—became models for aspiring writers. "Cry havoc" is found in in three of Shakespeare's plays: *King John* (1595), *Julius Caesar* (1601), and *Coriolanus* (1607). However, "wreak havoc" is not found in print before Christie's 1926 novel *The Murder of Roger Ackroyd*: "Annie is not allowed to wreak havoc with a dustpan and brush."

"Red neck."

ANNE NEWPORT ROYALL (1769–1854)

ARMERS WORKING LONG HOURS IN THE FIELDS ordinarily have a sunburned neck, as least on the back of the neck, the one part of their bodies exposed to the sun. The phrase was applied to the uneducated white farmer in the American South, especially share-croppers, and it was never meant as a compliment. "Red neck" might be compared to other put-downs such as "hillbilly," "hayseed," "white trash" and "wool hats" (in contrast to those who wore expensive silk hats). More recently, our phrase has been applied to white Southern conservatives by those who perceive them as reactionaries and bigots.

Author Anne Royall gave us the first published instance of the use of "red neck" in her 1830 narrative, *Southern Tour*:

> It must astonish everyone, after what I have said, (which is certainly no more than justice,) that I received but one dollar in Fayetteville! This may be ascribed to the Red Necks, a name bestowed upon the Presbyterians in Fayetteville. How many names these people have, matters not, for they still hoard money and you cannot shame them!

Later, in the early years of the nineteenth century, the political supporters of the Democratic Party in the South began to describe themselves as "red necks" and even wore red neckerchiefs to political rallies.

"*Been there, done that.*"

CYNTHIA LAUREN TEWES (1953–)

*A*CCORDING TO THE AUTHORITATIVE ON-LINE *PHRASE Finder*, the first appearance of this phrase in print appeared in a 1982 newspaper "Roving Reporter" article by Los Angeles journalist Jerry Buck. He had interviewed actress Lauren Tewes, then recently divorced, and had asked her if she was planning to remarry. Miss Tewes replied in the negative: "I've been there, done that." The answer means more than familiarity; it implies a negative attitude toward the subject under discussion—indifference to the point of repulsion.

Lauren Tewes is remembered primarily for her role as cruise director in the television situation comedy, *The Love Boat*.

Those interested (if there are any interested) should know that "Been There, Done That" tee-shirts are available from a number of sources.

"*Slippery slope.*"

JOAN FLEMING (1908–1980)

*M*OST OF US REALIZE THAT TAKING ONE SMALL STEP can lead to a chain of events out of all proportion to what we originally envisioned. The concept is sometimes referred to as "the domino effect," in which a long row of dominoes is toppled after the first in the line is pushed over. Logicians have found a serious fallacy in arguments that invoke the "slippery slope" unless the debater provides evidence that each step in the chain of events is actually a proven result of that first step.

Joan Fleming was a popular British novelist. Interestingly, her attraction to story-telling began with the bedtime tales she wove for her children, and she wrote several children's books before turning to adult fiction. The first popular use of our phrase in print is to be found in Fleming's 1951 novel, *The Man Who Looked Back* (where the slope is actually recommended: "You go off down the slippery slope. It'll do you good.")

And then there is the story of the inebriated gentleman who mistook the empty elevator shaft for the stairwell. His agonized warning to his companions was, "Watch that first step—it's a doozy!"

"The dustbin of history."

LEON TROTSKY (1879–1940)

*I*F WE ARE NOT BRITISH, WE MAY HAVE TO BE TOLD THAT Trotsky's "dustbin" is the American "garbage can." And so, to be tossed into a dustbin is to be thrown out with the rest of the trash—strong words.

Trotsky (born as Lev Bronshtein) was a Russian politician, Marxist revolutionary, and founder of the Red Army. He was a leader of the Bolsheviks in the civil war of 1918–1920. Trotsky's turbulent life ended in 1940 when he was assassinated in Mexico by agents of Joseph Stalin, the leader of the Soviet Union during the nineteen thirties and forties. When a minority party known s the "Mensheviks" walked out of the Second Congress of Soviets, Trotsky announced this: "You are pitiful, isolated individuals! You are bankrupts. Your role is played out. Go where you belong from now on—into the dustbin of history!"

A version of the "dustbin" phrase was used later by the American president Ronald Regan in 1982 in speaking before the British House of Commons: "Freedom and democracy will leave Marxism and Leninism on the ash heap of history." Libyan leader Muammar Gaddafi also used the phrase in a 2011 speech about countries attacking Libya: "This assault is by a bunch of fascists who will end up in the dustbin of history."

"*Don't go there.*"

GEORGE T. KEENEY (19?–)

THIS PIECE OF ADVICE IS HARDLY NOTEWORTHY IF WE TAKE the meaning it has always had until very recently. When asked, "Do you recommend Jack's Tavern?" the reply, "No. Don't go there," is completely straightforward. It wasn't until the nineteen-nineties that a new use for these words emerged. If Sally realizes her conversation with Jane is heading in a direction she is uncomfortable discussing, she might now say, "I guess Jack has his hobbies—don't go there."

George Keeney is an award winning chef whose popular column for the *Gettysburg Times*, "Ask the Chef," is the first printed source for this newer meaning. In the January 1997 number we find this exchange:

> Q: My biscuits seldom turn out thick and light. Most of the time they are like a hockey puck. Hey?
>
> A: It is a good thing I am a food service professional or I may be inclined to make a reference to the National Hockey League. (Don't go there).

Keeney did not reveal why the hockey league was not to be discussed. Perhaps it was nothing more than that the subject was irrelevant to the discussion of his questioner's cooking problems.

"*Break a leg!*"

EDNA FERBER (1885–1968)

*A*MONG THE TRADITIONS OF THE LEGITIMATE THEATER, the practice of sending a performer onto the stage with a cheery "Break a leg!" may seem strange to the layman, but our superstitious actors and musicians believe that wishing someone "Good luck!" is bad luck and bad manners. A competent performer does not need luck to succeed, and the wishing them luck contradicts that idea, or so stage performers have always thought.

The "break a leg" wish has come into popular use outside of the theatrical world, and it is now not uncommon to hear it offered to public speakers, business sales presenters, and on many other occasions where someone must face a live audience.

Edna Ferber was an award-winning American author of novels, stories, and plays, and is probably best remembered for her 1926 novel *Show Boat* and its subsequent stage and film versions. The earliest example of "Break a leg!" in print will be found in Ferber's *A Peculiar Treasure* (1939) in which our demand for a bone fracture is turned around: "All the understudies sat in the back row politely wishing the various principals would break a leg."

"Down the tubes."

WILLIAM PARRY O'BRIEN, JR. (1932–2007)

O'BRIEN WAS AN AMERICAN TRACK AND FIELD CHAMPION. He won two gold medals in the Olympics in the shot put (1952 and 1956) and in 1984 was inducted into the United States Olympics Hall of Fame. O'Brien developed a new technique for the event, facing away from the target area and spinning one-hundred eighty degrees to throw the shot with greater forward momentum than previous shot putters. With this method he won one-hundred sixteen consecutive meets while setting a new world record for distance seventeen times.

After retirement, when one of his records had been broken, O'Brien was quoted as follows: "I was proud of that record. Then I had visions of all my records going down the tubes."

This brings us to a question: "What tubes did he mean?" We have toothpaste tubes, vacuum tubes, mailing tubes, the tube in London (that is, the subway), inner tubes, the television tube (or "boob tube"), and test tubes. None of these seem to match what O'Brien might have meant. He must have been referring to the pipes through which lavatory waste is conveyed to our sewers, and thus his statement is the equivalent of a more familiar, "Visions of all my records going down the drain."

"Catch 22."

JOSEPH HELLER (1923–1999)

*W*HEN FRIENDS REACH A DEAD END IN THEIR LIVES, OR when either of two alternatives are losers for them we often say "Damned if you do and damned if you don't" or "Heads I win, tails you lose," or it is "a no-win situation" or "a vicious circle." We might even say, "That's a catch 22" where "catch" has the meaning of a hidden problem in something that looks very good on the surface (as in "there must be a *catch* to it"). But author Heller's "Catch 22" is a much more complicated idea.

His novel *Catch 22* took eight years to complete. The key idea revolved around the possibility of Air Force pilots being relieved from flying combat missions due to insanity. The catch was that pilot who has had numerous close calls would be crazy not to ask to be grounded. However, making such a request was seen as proof of sanity. Yes, it was a trap.

Trivia buffs should know that Heller's first title for the story was *Catch 18.*

"Dumb ox."

THOMAS AQUINAS (1225–1274)

OR THE RECORD, THOMAS AQUINAS DID NOT ORIGINATE this phrase. It was the nickname his fellow students gave him because as a youngster he was a very fat and a very unresponsive pupil. However, their teacher, Albert of Cologne (now remembered as "Albert the Great") contradicted them: "You call him a Dumb Ox; I tell you this Dumb Ox shall bellow so loud that his bellowings will fill the world." Indeed, a popular biography of Thomas by the British journalist-philosopher G.K. Chesterton was entitled, *St. Thomas Aquinas, the Dumb Ox* (1923).

Thomas's bellowings did fill the world. Much of our contemporary philosophy either develops his ideas or contradicts them, especially in the areas of ethics, aesthetics (or the theory of art), and political theory, and to this day the Catholic Church considers him its greatest theologian and philosopher.

As a phrase, "dumb ox" suggests our word "lummox" for a stupid and clumsy person, apparently formed from the two words "lumbering" and "ox."

"Beat the living daylights out of..."

HENRY FIELDING (1707–1754)

*I*F YOU BEAT THE LIVING DAYLIGHTS OUT OF SOMEONE, WHAT exactly does your victim lose? What are these "daylights"? Though we no longer use this meaning, "daylights" once meant "eyes." And so our phrase is much like today's "I'll put his lights out," meaning to knock someone unconscious.

Henry Fielding was an English novelist and playwright, remembered today especially for his 1749 novel *The History of Tom Jones, a Foundling* (usually referenced more simply as *Tom Jones*). It is in his 1752 Novel *Amelia* that we find the first published appearance of our "daylights" as someone's eyes: "Good woman! I don't use to be so treated. If the lady says such another word to me, d--n me, I will darken her daylights."

Last, we note that *The Living Daylights* was the title for the fifteenth James Bond movie and the first of these to star British actor Timothy Dolton. The plot for the film was based on a short story by British author Ian Fleming, the creator of the popular series of books and stories about his illustrious British secret agent, James Bond.

"Back-seat driver."

PELHAM GRENVILLE WODEHOUSE (1881–1975)

P.G. WODEHOUSE WAS AN ENGLISH AUTHOR, HUMORIST, and poet who is most remembered for his series of stories featuring Bertie Wooster and his butler Jeeves. We have forgotten that Wodehouse was also a successful playwright and songwriter. He credits include fifteen plays and two-hundred fifty popular song lyrics including the hit song "Bill," which was featured in Jerome Kern's 1927 theatrical masterpiece *Show Boat*. Wodehouse was inducted into the Songwriters Hall of Fame in 1975.

A "back-seat driver" is shorthand for the kind of automobile passenger who offers unsolicited advice (including a stream of negative criticism) to the person behind the wheel. The first published instance of the phrase is to be found in Wodehouse's 1930 novel *Very Good, Jeeves!*— "Quite suddenly and unexpectedly, no one more surprised than myself, the car let out a faint gurgle like a sick moose and stopped in its tracks. The back-seat drivers gave tongue. 'What's the matter? What has happened?'"

Wodehouse is still read and enjoyed today. This is especially true of his Bertie and Jeeves stories and novels which, though built around the world of the upper-class in England before World War I, are still found entertaining. In fact, a British television series adapted from these stories and which aired on PBS in the United States in the nineteen-nineties brought Wodehouse's work to a vast new audience.

"*Have an axe to grind.*"

CHARLES MINER (1780–1865)

*I*T IS SURPRISING WHEN WE THINK OF THE NUMBER OF expressions in use in today's industrialized and digitalized world that harken back to the era of the farm and the forest. As one example of many, we say that a corporation that receives a surprise in the form of unforeseen and perhaps unearned income has enjoyed "windfall profits." The phrase was derived from the apple orchard when the wind blew a ripe apple from the tree and this "windfall" was much easier to claim than those apples that could not be enjoyed without a ladder or the ability to climb the tree.

The axe that we have to grind is our own private agenda behind the position we take in a discussion or argument. If we argue against a new housing development on principle, our sincerity may be called into question if it is known that our own property's value will suffer or that we have an interest in a rival development. In other words, we have an ulterior motive.

Charles Minor was the publisher of the *Luzerne County Federalist* in Wilkes-Barre, Pennsylvania. His 1810 story, 'Who'll Turn the Grindstone,"—about a youngster who was tricked into turning a grindstone for a stranger who had an axe to grind—is the first known instance of the use of our phrase in print.

"*Vanity plates.*"

BARBARA ELIZABETH LININGTON (1921–1988)

I RUMBA. OOO GAH. O BEANS. GIMME 5. LQQKIE.

RIVING AN AUTOMOBILE THESE DAYS MEANS NOTICING license plates that do much more than identify the vehicle and announce that applicable taxes have been paid. There are also very brief but still decipherable messages: greetings, insults, boasts, and other notices of every conceivable kind. Some commentators have the opinion that these so-called "vanity plates" are a form of graffiti and a way of getting "one-up" on other drivers. But a better answer may be that we all dislike being assigned an anonymous and random ID number, and "vanity plates" are one way to escape that indignity.

Barbara Linington was an award-winning American author of crime novels, especially novels that are called "police procedurals"— stories that follow the movements of detectives investigating a crime and especially a sensational crime. Linington was the first woman author to succeed at procedurals, a category of detective fiction that had been an exclusively male writer's field. The first published reference to "vanity plates" will be found in Linington's 1975 *Crime File* (written under the penname "D. Shannon"): "The drivers who wanted to pay extra could buy the vanity plates."

"You could look it up."

BIBLIOGRAPHY

><s PRIMARY SOURCE

Oxford English Dictionary. 2nd edition, twenty volumes, New York: Oxford University Press USA, 1989.

><s SUPPLEMENTARY SOURCES

Ammer, Christine. *Have a Nice Day! No Problem! A Dictionary of Clichés.* New York: Plume Books, 1992.

Auden, W.H. and Louis Kronenberger. *The Viking Book of Aphorisms: A Personal Selection.* New York: Viking, 1981.

Beale, Paul. *Partridge's Concise Dictionary of Slang and Unconventional English: From the Work of Eric Partridge.* New York: Macmillan, 1989.

Evans, Ivor H., Editor. *Brewer's Dictionary of Phrase and Fable.* Fourteenth Edition, New York: Harper and Row, 1989.

Henderson, Robert. *The Facts on File Encyclopedia of Word and Phrase Origins.* New York: Facts on File Publications, 1987.

Keyes, Ralph. *"Nice Guys Finish Seventh": False Phrases, Spurious Sayings, and Familiar Misquotations.* New York: Harper Perennial, 1992.

Kirkpatrick, Betty. *Clichés: Over 1500 Phrases Explored and Explained.* New York: St. Martin's Griffin, 1996.

Partridge, Eric. *A Dictionary of Catch Phrases: American and British, from the Sixteenth Century to the Present Day.* New York: Stein & Day, 1977.

Pickering, Davis, et al. *Brewer's Dictionary of Twentieth-Century Phrase and Fable.* Boston: Houghton Mifflin, 1992.

Rogers, James. *The Dictionary of Clichés.* New York: Harper Perennial, 1985.

Why Do We Say it? The Stories Behind the Words, Expressions and Clichés We Use. Secaucus, New Jersey: Castle Books, 1984.

✍ ON THE WEB

Phrase Finder. (http://www.phrases.org.uk/meanings/index.html)

Wikipedia. (http://en.wikipedia.org/wiki)

Project Gutenberg (http://www.gutenberg.org/)

www.ingramcontent.com/pod-product-compliance
Lightning Source LLC
Chambersburg PA
CBHW070901290526
45795CB00001B/192